HOME BAKING

HOME BAKING

Home-made treats for the whole family

This edition published by Parragon Books Ltd in 2013
LOVE FOOD is an imprint of Parragon Books Ltd

Parragon Books Ltd
Chartist House
15–17 Trim Street
Bath BA1 1HA, UK
www.parragon.com/lovefood

ISBN: 978-1-4723-2346-0

Printed in China

Notes for the Reader

This book uses both metric and imperial measurements. Follow the
same units of measurement throughout; do not mix metric and
imperial. All spoon measurements are level: teaspoons are assumed to
be 5 ml, and tablespoons are assumed to be 15 ml. Unless otherwise
stated, milk is assumed to be full fat, eggs and individual vegetables are
medium, and pepper is freshly ground black pepper.

Garnishes, decorations and serving suggestions are all optional and not
necessarily included in the recipe ingredients or method.

The times given are an approximate guide only. Preparation times differ
according to the techniques used by different people and the cooking
times may also vary from those given. Optional ingredients, variations
or serving suggestions have not been included in the time calculations.

Recipes using raw or very lightly cooked eggs should be avoided by
infants, the elderly, pregnant women, convalescents and anyone suffering
from an illness. Pregnant and breastfeeding women are advised to avoid
eating peanuts and peanut products. Sufferers from nut allergies should
be aware that some of the ready-made ingredients used in the recipes
in this book may contain nuts. Always check the packaging before use.

Contents

Introduction

From a plate of simple biscuits to a moist and indulgent chocolate cake, or a delicious fruit pie, nothing can beat the flavour of home baked treats. The wonderful aroma that fills the air from a warm kitchen and the satisfaction of presenting your own creation to family or friends is so rewarding that it's no wonder that home baking is more popular now than ever before.

This book contains a collection of traditional recipes that are easy to make with clear instructions and simple decorations. Whether it's for a mid-morning coffee, afternoon tea, a birthday treat or a special celebration, you'll find a dish to fit the occasion.

The Basic Ingredients

As with any type of cooking it's worth buying good quality basic ingredients. For the best flavour, choose a lightly salted or unsalted butter. Soft margarine can be used instead of butter, but avoid low fat spreads as they have a high water content and an inferior taste.

Always use the correct-sized egg. Unless specified, all the recipes in this book use medium eggs. Allow the eggs to come to room temperature for about 1 hour before using.

Check that flours and raising agents are not past their sell by date. Stale flour will impart an unpleasant taste and raising agents can lose their effectiveness resulting in heavy-textured cakes.

Caster sugar is the most popular sugar for cake making – its fine grains dissolve easily when creamed with butter. To make your own vanilla sugar, simply pop a vanilla pod in a container of caster sugar and leave for 5–6 days. Chocolate and darker fruit cakes are often made with soft brown sugars or unrefined muscovado sugar as they give a richer colour and flavour.

Essential Equipment

Any reasonably equipped kitchen should have most of the basics needed for cake making – bowls, spoons, spatulas, a sieve and a wire rack for cooling. A good set of measuring scales to ensure accurate weighing is also essential and a handheld electric mixer will make light work of creaming and whisking.

The only other major items to buy are the appropriate-sized baking tins. You'll need a range of shapes and sizes so you'll probably have to build up your collection gradually. When buying, pick sturdy tins that will last – flimsy tins may buckle quickly and have to be replaced. If you buy tins with a non-stick coating, take care not to scratch the lining with metal utensils. Always wash tins thoroughly after use and place in a warm oven to dry out completely before putting away. An alternative to metal tins is to try flexible non-stick silicone bakeware – you'll find a good range of shapes, sizes and colours and they are easy to use and clean.

Secrets of Success

Always read the recipe before you start baking. Make sure that you have all the ingredients to hand (at room temperature, if necessary). Weigh out the ingredients accurately – this is especially important with raising agents, such as baking powder or bicarbonate of soda, as too much or too little can have a drastic effect on the finished cake.

Before turning on the oven, make sure the shelves are in the correct position. Allow at least 10 minutes for the oven to preheat to the required temperature. If you have a fan oven check the manufacturers' instructions – you may need to reduce the temperature by 10–20°C/50–68°F. Once the cake is in the oven, don't be tempted to open the door too soon or too often as the cold air will lower the temperature and the cake may sink.
Take time to prepare the correct-sized baking tin. Lightly grease with melted butter or a flavourless cooking oil then line with baking paper, cutting to fit neatly.

There are two ways to test whether a cake is cooked. For a light sponge cake, simply press the top of the cake gently with your fingertips. The cake should feel springy to the touch and give very lightly, leaving no imprint. For richer cakes or fruit cakes, it's best to insert a thin skewer into the centre of the cake, then pull it out quickly – the skewer should come away clean. If there is any cake mixture sticking to the skewer then return the cake to the oven and bake for a little longer.

Freshly baked cakes and biscuits are very fragile so leave them to cool in the tin for 5–15 minutes before turning them out. Run a thin-bladed palette knife around the edge of the tin to loosen the cake before inverting onto a wire rack. To prevent marks on the top of delicate sponges, quickly flip them onto another rack. Let very crumbly bars cool completely in the tin before turning out.

Common Cake Dilemmas

- If the cake has sunk in the middle – has too much raising agent been used, the oven door been opened too soon or the cake not been cooked for long enough?

- If the cake has a dry and crumbly texture – has the cake been cooked for too long or has too much baking powder been used?

- If the cake has not risen – has not enough raising agent been used or has the cake mixture been over-whisked/beaten?

- Always make sure the cake is completely cold before storing it in an airtight tin. If the cake is still a little warm, condensation may form which can cause mould to grow on the surface.

- If the cake has a fresh cream or soft cheese filling or icing, it will need to be stored in the refrigerator but allow it to stand at room temperature for about 30 minutes before serving.

- Some cakes will improve in flavour if kept for a few days before serving. Wrap well in greaseproof paper and then foil to prevent them from drying out.

- Many cakes freeze well. Place in large freezer bags or wrap in foil, excluding as much air as possible. Unwrap before defrosting and leave at room temperature to defrost thoroughly.

Brownies & Bars

Black & White Brownies

Makes 24 brownies

Chocolate Mixture

350 g/12 oz plain chocolate, broken into pieces

115 g/4 oz butter, plus extra for greasing

6 eggs

450 g/1 lb caster sugar

175 g/6 oz plain flour

1½ tsp baking powder

1½ tsp salt

1½ tsp vanilla extract

1 tsp almond extract

Cream Cheese Mixture

85 g/3 oz butter

225 g/8 oz cream cheese

150 g/5½ oz caster sugar

3 eggs

25 g/1 oz plain flour

1 tsp vanilla extract

Directions

• Preheat the oven to 180°C/350°F/Gas Mark 4.

• Grease a 33 x 23-cm/13 x 9-inch baking tin.

• Prepare the chocolate mixture. Slowly melt the chocolate and the butter in a heatproof bowl placed over a pan of gently simmering water. Mix well and set aside to cool.

• Whip the eggs and caster sugar until fluffy in a separate bowl. Stir the flour, baking powder and salt together and mix into the egg mixture. Mix in the melted chocolate and butter, then add the vanilla and almond extract.

• To make the cream cheese mixture, cream the butter in a bowl, then add the cream cheese and caster sugar. Beat until fluffy and add in the eggs, then the flour and vanilla extract.

• Spread half the chocolate mixture in the tin, then spread with the cream cheese mixture. Spoon the remaining chocolate mixture on top. Swirl the two mixtures together with a knife.

• Bake in the preheated oven for 40 minutes. Leave to cool and cut into bars.

Double Chocolate Brownies

Makes 16 brownies

Ingredients

115 g/4 oz butter, plus extra for greasing

115 g/4 oz plain chocolate, broken into pieces

275 g/9¾ oz caster sugar

Pinch of salt

1 tsp vanilla extract

2 eggs

115 g/4 oz plain flour

2 tbsp cocoa powder

85 g/3 oz white chocolate chips

Fudge Sauce

55 g/2 oz butter

200 g/7 oz caster sugar

150 ml/5 fl oz milk

225 ml/8 fl oz double cream

150 g/5½ oz golden syrup

175 g/6 oz plain chocolate, broken into pieces

Directions

• Preheat the oven to 180°C/350°F/Gas Mark 4.

• Grease a 20-cm/8-inch square cake tin and line the base with baking paper.

• Place the butter and chocolate in a small heatproof bowl set over a saucepan of gently simmering water until melted. Stir until smooth. Leave to cool slightly then pour into a larger mixing bowl. Stir in the caster sugar, salt and vanilla extract. Add the eggs, one at a time, stirring well, until blended.

• Sift the flour and cocoa into the cake mixture and beat until smooth. Stir in the chocolate chips, then pour the mixture into the prepared tin.

• Bake in the preheated oven for 35–40 minutes or until the top is evenly coloured and a skewer inserted into the centre comes out almost clean. Leave to cool slightly while you prepare the sauce.

• To make the fudge sauce, place the butter, caster sugar, milk, cream and golden syrup in a small saucepan and heat gently until the sugar has dissolved. Bring to the boil and stir for 10 minutes or until the mixture is caramel-coloured. Remove from the heat and add the chocolate. Stir until smooth. Cut the brownies into squares and serve immediately with the sauce.

Almond & Raspberry Bars

Makes 12 bars

Pastry Base

175 g/6 oz plain flour

115 g/4 oz butter, plus extra for greasing

25 g/1 oz caster sugar

1 egg yolk

1 tbsp ice-cold water

Filling

115 g/4 oz butter

100 g/3½ oz caster sugar

100 g/3½ oz ground almonds

3 eggs, beaten

½ tsp almond extract

4 tbsp raspberry jam

2 tbsp flaked almonds

Directions

• Preheat the oven to 200°C/400°F/Gas Mark 6.

• Grease a 23-cm/9-inch square cake tin.

• For the pastry base, sift the flour into a bowl and rub in the butter with your fingertips until the mixture resembles fine breadcrumbs. Stir in the sugar, then combine the egg yolk and water and stir in to make a firm dough, adding a little more water if necessary. Wrap in clingfilm and chill in the refrigerator for about 15 minutes until firm enough to roll out.

• Roll out the dough and line the base and sides of the cake tin. Prick the base and chill for 15 minutes.

• For the filling, cream the butter and caster sugar together until pale and fluffy, then beat in the ground almonds, eggs and almond extract.

• Spread the jam over the base, then top with the almond filling, spreading it evenly. Sprinkle with the flaked almonds.

• Bake in the preheated oven for 10 minutes, then reduce the temperature to 180°C/350°F/Gas Mark 4 and bake for a further 25–30 minutes or until the filling is golden brown and firm to the touch. Cool in the tin, then cut into bars.

Lemon Drizzle Bars

Makes 12 bars

Ingredients

2 eggs

140 g/5 oz caster sugar

140 g/5 oz soft margarine, plus extra
for greasing

Finely grated rind of 1 lemon

175 g/6 oz self-raising flour

125 ml/4 fl oz milk

Syrup

150 g/5½ oz icing sugar, plus extra
for dusting

4 tbsp fresh lemon juice

Directions

• Preheat the oven to 180°C/350°F/Gas Mark 4.

• Grease a 20-cm/8-inch square cake tin and line with baking paper.

• Place the eggs, caster sugar and margarine in a bowl and beat well until smooth and fluffy. Stir in the lemon rind, then fold in the flour lightly and evenly. Stir in the milk, mixing evenly, then spoon the mixture into the prepared cake tin, smoothing level.

• Bake in the preheated oven for 45–50 minutes, or until golden brown and firm to the touch. Remove from the oven and place the tin on a wire rack.

• To make the syrup, place the icing sugar and lemon juice in a small saucepan and heat gently, stirring until the sugar dissolves. Do not boil.

• Prick the warm cake all over with a skewer and spoon the hot syrup evenly over the top.

• Leave to cool completely in the tin, then turn out the cake, cut into 12 pieces and dust with a little icing sugar before serving.

Brownies & Bars 17

Trail Mix Bars

Makes 16 bars

Ingredients

175 g/6 oz margarine, plus extra

  for greasing

3 tbsp clear honey

175 g/6 oz soft light brown sugar

125 g/4½ oz smooth peanut butter

275 g/9¾ oz porridge oats

35 g/1¼ oz dried apricots, chopped

2 tbsp vegetable oil

2 tbsp sesame seeds

Directions

• Preheat the oven to 180°C/350°F/Gas Mark 4.

• Grease and line a 23-cm/9-inch square baking tin with baking paper.

• Melt the margarine, honey and brown sugar in a saucepan over a low heat. When the sugar has dissolved, add the peanut butter and stir until everything is well combined.

• Add the oats, apricots, vegetable oil and sesame seeds and mix well.

• Press the mixture into the prepared tin and bake in the preheated oven for 20 minutes or until golden brown.

• Remove from the oven and leave to cool in the tin, then cut into 16 squares and serve.

Cinnamon Raisin Bars

Makes 16 bars

Base

115 g/4 oz butter, plus extra for greasing

225 g/8 oz soft light brown sugar

175 g/6 oz plain flour

1 egg

140 g/5 oz porridge oats

½ tsp bicarbonate of soda

½ tsp salt

2 tbsp water

Raisin Filling

55 g/2 oz caster sugar

1 tsp ground cinnamon

1 tbsp cornflour

225 ml/8 fl oz water

300 g/10½ oz raisins

Directions

- Preheat the oven to 180°C/350°F/Gas Mark 4.

- Grease a 33 x 23 x 5-cm/13 x 9 x 2-inch baking tin.

- To make the base, cream together the butter and brown sugar in a mixing bowl. Set aside.

- Combine the flour, egg, oats, bicarbonate of soda and salt in a separate bowl. Add the mixture to the creamed butter and sugar mix. Stir together with the water and beat until crumbly.

- Spoon half of the mixture into the baking tin, pressing it firmly into place with the back of a spoon.

- To make the filling, combine the caster sugar, cinnamon, cornflour and water in a saucepan and stir until smooth. Add the raisins. Cook the mixture over a medium heat until it is thick and bubbly.

- Leave to cool to room temperature, then spread the filling over the base. Top the filling with the remaining oat mixture and press down firmly.

- Bake in the preheated oven for 30–35 minutes or until golden brown. Leave to cool on a wire rack. Cut into bars once cold.

Chocolate Fudge Brownies

Makes 9 brownies

Ingredients

225 g/8 oz plain chocolate, broken into pieces

115 g/4 oz butter, plus extra for greasing

200 g/7 oz caster sugar

Pinch of salt

2 tbsp water

2 large eggs

1 tsp vanilla extract

100 g/3½ oz plain flour

55 g/2 oz walnuts, chopped (optional)

icing sugar, for dusting (optional)

Directions

• Preheat the oven to 160°C/325°F/Gas Mark 3.

• Grease a 20-cm/8-inch square baking tin and line the base with baking paper.

• Place the chocolate, butter, caster sugar, salt and water in small saucepan over a very low heat. Heat, stirring often, until the chocolate and butter are melted and the sugar is dissolved.

• Pour into a mixing bowl. Stir in the eggs, one at a time. Stir in the vanilla extract. Stir in the flour. Fold in the nuts if using.

• Pour the mixture into the prepared tin.

• Bake in the preheated oven for 35 minutes. Leave to cool completely before cutting into 9 squares.

• Dust with icing sugar if desired.

Cranberry Soured Cream Brownies

Makes 12 brownies

Ingredients

115 g/4 oz butter, plus extra for greasing

4 tbsp cocoa powder

225 g/8 oz soft dark brown sugar

115 g/4 oz self-raising flour

2 eggs, lightly beaten

125 g/4½ oz fresh cranberries

Topping

150 g/5½ oz soured cream or crème fraîche

1 tbsp caster sugar

1 tbsp self-raising flour

1 egg yolk

½ tsp vanilla extract

Directions

• Preheat the oven to 180°C/350°F/Gas Mark 4.

• Grease and lightly flour a shallow 33 x 23-cm/ 13 x 9-inch baking tin.

• Place the butter, cocoa and brown sugar in a saucepan and stir over a low heat until just melted. Leave to cool slightly. Quickly stir in the flour and eggs and beat hard until thoroughly mixed to a smooth mixture. Stir in the cranberries.

• Spread the mixture into the baking tin.

• To make the topping, place all the ingredients in a bowl and beat together until smooth. Spoon over the chocolate mixture, swirling evenly with a palette knife.

• Bake in the preheated oven for 35–40 minutes or until risen and firm.

• Leave to cool in the tin, then cut into squares.

Apricot Bars

Makes 10 bars

Ingredients

175 g/6 oz butter, plus extra for greasing

100 g/3½ oz soft light brown sugar

4 tbsp clear honey

100 g/3½ oz dried apricots, chopped

2 tsp sesame seeds

225 g/8 oz porridge oats

Directions

• Preheat the oven to 180°C/350°F/Gas Mark 4.

• Very lightly grease a shallow 28 x 18-cm/11 x 7-inch baking tin.

• Place the butter, brown sugar and honey in a small saucepan over a low heat and heat until the ingredients have melted together.

• Stir the apricots, sesame seeds and oats into the mixture, then spoon into the prepared tin and lightly smooth the top.

• Bake in the preheated oven for 20–25 minutes or until golden brown.

• Cut into 10 bars and leave to cool completely in the tin.

Nutty Granola Bars

Makes 16 bars

Ingredients

225 g/8 oz porridge oats

85 g/3 oz hazelnuts, chopped

55 g/2 oz plain flour

115 g/4 oz butter, plus extra for greasing

2 tbsp golden syrup

115 g/4 oz soft light brown sugar

Directions

• Preheat the oven to 180°C/350°F/Gas Mark 4.

• Grease a 23-cm/9-inch square cake tin.

• Place the oats, hazelnuts and flour in a large bowl and stir together.

• Place the butter, golden syrup and brown sugar in a saucepan over a low heat and stir until the butter has melted and the sugar is dissolved.

• Pour the melted mixture over the dry ingredients and mix well.

• Spoon the mixture into the tin and smooth the top.

• Bake in the preheated oven for 20–25 minutes or until golden and firm to the touch.

• Cut into 16 pieces and leave to cool in the tin.

Chocolate Peppermint Bars

Makes 16 bars

Base

55 g/2 oz butter, plus extra for greasing

55 g/2 oz caster sugar

100 g/3½ oz plain flour

Filling

175 g/6 oz icing sugar

1–2 tbsp warm water

½ tsp peppermint extract

2 tsp green food colouring (optional)

Topping

175 g/6 oz plain chocolate, broken

into pieces

Directions

• Preheat the oven to 180°C/350°F/Gas Mark 4.

• Grease and line a 33 x 23-cm/13 x 9-inch baking tin with baking paper.

• Place the butter and caster sugar in a large bowl and beat together until light and fluffy. Stir in the flour until the mixture binds together.

• Knead the mixture to form a smooth dough, then press into the tin and prick the surface all over with a fork. Bake in the preheated oven for 10–15 minutes, or until lightly browned and just firm to the touch. Leave to cool in the tin.

• To make the filling, sift the sugar into a bowl. Gradually add the water, then add the peppermint extract and food colouring if using. Spread the filling over the base, then leave to set.

• To make the topping, place the chocolate in a heatproof bowl, set the bowl over a saucepan of gently simmering water and heat until melted. Spread the chocolate over the filling, then leave to set in the refrigerator for at least an hour.

• Cut into bars and serve.

Sticky Pecan Pie Bars

Makes 10 bars

Base

150 g/5½ oz plain flour

55 g/2 oz butter, plus extra for greasing

55 g/2 oz soft light brown sugar

Topping

2 large eggs

115 g/4 oz soft light brown sugar

40 g/1½ oz pecan nuts, chopped

85 g/3 oz butter, melted

115 g/4 oz golden syrup

½ tsp vanilla extract

Directions

• Preheat the oven to 190°C/375°F/Gas Mark 5.

• Line a shallow 23-cm/9-inch square baking tin with baking paper and grease the paper.

• To make the base, place the flour and butter, cut into cubes, in a large bowl and rub the butter in with your fingertips until the mixture resembles fine breadcrumbs. Stir in the brown sugar. Spoon the mixture into the tin and press down firmly with the back of a spoon. Bake in the preheated oven for 20 minutes.

• Meanwhile, to make the topping, place the eggs in a large bowl and beat lightly. Add the brown sugar, the pecan nuts, melted butter, golden syrup and vanilla extract and stir together until combined.

• Pour the mixture over the base in the tin and bake in the preheated oven for a further 15–20 minutes, or until firm to the touch and golden brown. Remove from the tin and leave to cool. When cold, cut into 10 bars to serve.

Apple & Cinnamon Bars

Makes 14 bars

Base

115 g/4 oz unsalted butter, plus extra

for greasing

115 g/4 oz caster sugar

1 tsp vanilla extract

2 eggs, beaten

115 g/4 oz plain flour

2 large cooking apples

2 tbsp lemon juice

Topping

55 g/2 oz blanched almonds, finely chopped

30 g/1 oz plain flour

55 g/2 oz soft light brown sugar

½ tsp ground cinnamon

25 g/1 oz unsalted butter, melted

Directions

- Preheat the oven to 180°C/350°F/Gas Mark 4.

- Grease and line a 28 x 18-cm/11 x 7-inch cake tin.

- Cream the butter, caster sugar and vanilla extract together until pale. Gradually add the eggs, beating thoroughly. Sift in the flour and fold in evenly.

- Prepare the apples by peeling, dicing and sprinkling with lemon juice. Add to the flour mixture and mix.

- Spread the mixture into the base of the cake tin. Press the mixture down with the back of a wooden spoon or palette knife.

- For the topping, mix all the ingredients to a crumbly texture and sprinkle over the cake. Bake in the preheated oven for 45–55 minutes until firm and golden.

- Cut into bars and serve warm or cooled.

No-Bake Chocolate Fingers

Makes 14 bars

Ingredients

175 g/6 oz plain chocolate, broken into pieces

55 g/2 oz butter, plus extra for greasing

2 tbsp golden syrup

115 g/4 oz digestive biscuits, broken
  into pieces

225 g/8 oz mixed dried fruit

55 g/2 oz glacé cherries

Directions

• Grease a 28 x 18-cm/11 x 7-inch cake tin and line with baking paper.

• Place the chocolate in a heatproof bowl, set the bowl over a saucepan of gently simmering water and heat until melted.

• Add the butter and golden syrup and stir until well combined. Remove from the heat.

• Stir the biscuit pieces into the melted chocolate mixture, along with the dried fruit and cherries.

• Pour the chocolate mixture into the tin, pressing down well with the back of a spoon. Chill in the refrigerator for 2 hours or until firm.

• Cut into 14 fingers to serve.

Chocolate Oat Bars

Makes 16 bars

Ingredients

115 g/4 oz plain flour

90 g/3¼ oz porridge oats

175 g/6 oz soft light brown sugar

115 g/4 oz butter, plus extra for greasing

Filling

½ tsp vanilla extract

400 g/14 oz can sweetened condensed milk

115 g/4 oz nuts, chopped

175 g/6 oz plain chocolate chips

Directions

• Preheat the oven to 180°C/350°F/Gas Mark 4.

• Grease a 33 x 23-cm/13 x 9-inch baking tin.

• Combine the flour, oats, brown sugar and butter in a large bowl, mixing them together well. Reserve 85 g/ 3 oz of the oat mixture. Press the remainder of the mixture into the base of the prepared tin.

• Bake in the preheated oven for 10 minutes.

• Mix the vanilla extract into the condensed milk and pour this over the baked base. Sprinkle with the nuts and the chocolate chips.

• Top with the remaining oat mixture and press down firmly.

• Bake for a further 25-30 minutes or until lightly browned. Cool and cut into bars.

Marshmallow Crunch Bars

Makes 8 bars

Ingredients

175 g/6 oz plain flour

1 tbsp baking powder

175 g/6 oz unsalted butter, softened, plus
   extra for greasing

150 g/5½ oz caster sugar

3 eggs beaten

1 tsp vanilla extract

55 g/2 oz mixed nuts, chopped

30 g/1 oz mini marshmallows

60 g/2¼ oz glacé cherries, chopped

Directions

• Preheat the oven to 180°C/350°F/Gas Mark 4.

• Grease a 23-cm/9-inch square baking tin.

• Combine the flour and baking powder in a large bowl
  and add the butter, caster sugar, eggs and vanilla extract.
  Beat well until the mixture is smooth.

• Stir two thirds of the nuts, marshmallows and chopped
  cherries into the mixture.

• Spoon into the prepared tin and smooth the top with a
  palette knife. Sprinkle the remaining nuts, marshmallows
  and cherries on top.

• Bake in the preheated oven for 40–50 minutes or
  until lightly browned. Cool in the tin for 20 minutes
  until firm, then cut into bars, and finish cooling on a
  wire rack.

Biscuits
& Cookies

Peanut Butter Biscuits

Makes about 26 biscuits

Ingredients

115 g/4 oz butter, softened

125 g/4½ oz crunchy peanut butter

100 g/3½ oz caster sugar

115 g/4 oz soft light brown sugar

1 egg, beaten

½ tsp vanilla extract

85 g/3 oz plain flour

½ tsp bicarbonate of soda

½ tsp baking powder

Pinch of salt

140 g/5 oz porridge oats

Directions

• Preheat the oven to 180°C/350°F/Gas Mark 4.

• Line several baking trays with baking paper.

• Place the butter and peanut butter in a bowl and beat together. Beat in the caster sugar and brown sugar, then gradually beat in the egg and vanilla extract.

• Sift the flour, bicarbonate of soda, baking powder and salt into the bowl and stir in the oats.

• Place spoonfuls of the biscuit mixture on to the baking trays, spaced well apart to allow for spreading. Flatten slightly with a fork.

• Bake in the preheated oven for 12 minutes or until lightly browned.

• Leave to cool on the baking trays for 2 minutes, then transfer to wire racks to cool completely.

Oatmeal, Raisin & Nut Biscuits

Makes about 30 biscuits

Ingredients

85 g/3 oz raisins, chopped

125 ml/4 fl oz orange juice

225 g/8 oz butter, softened

150 g/5½ oz caster sugar

1 egg yolk, lightly beaten

2 tsp vanilla extract

225 g/8 oz plain flour

Pinch of salt

50 g/1¾ oz porridge oats

55 g/2 oz hazelnuts, chopped

Whole hazelnuts, to decorate

Directions

• Preheat the oven to 190°C/375°F/Gas Mark 5.

• Line several baking trays with baking paper.

• Put the raisins in a bowl, add the orange juice and leave to soak for 10 minutes.

• Put the butter and caster sugar into a large bowl and mix well with a wooden spoon, then beat in the egg yolk and vanilla extract. Sift the flour and salt into the mixture and add the oats and chopped hazelnuts. Drain the raisins, discarding the orange juice. Add the raisins to the mixture and stir until thoroughly combined.

• Drop dessertspoonfuls of the mixture on to the prepared baking trays, spaced well apart. Flatten slightly and place a whole hazelnut in the centre of each biscuit.

• Bake in the preheated oven for 12–15 minutes until golden brown. Leave to cool on the baking trays for 5–10 minutes, then carefully transfer the biscuits to wire racks to cool completely.

Vanilla Sugar Biscuits

Makes about 12 biscuits

Ingredients

175 g/6 oz plain flour

175 g/6 oz butter, cut into pieces

200 g/7 oz caster sugar, plus extra
   for dusting

1 tsp vanilla extract

Directions

• Preheat the oven to 180°C/350°F/Gas Mark 4.

• Line several baking trays with baking paper.

• Sift the flour into a large bowl. Add the butter and rub it in with your fingertips until the mixture resembles fine breadcrumbs. Stir in the caster sugar and vanilla extract and mix together to form a firm dough.

• Roll out the dough on a lightly floured work surface to a thickness of 1 cm/½ inch. Stamp out 12 hearts with a heart-shaped biscuit cutter. Arrange the hearts on the prepared baking tray.

• Bake in the preheated oven for 15–20 minutes or until just coloured. Transfer to a wire rack and leave to cool completely.

• Dust with a little sugar just before serving.

Blueberry & Cranberry Biscuits

Makes about 30 biscuits

Ingredients

225 g/8 oz butter, softened

150 g/5½ oz caster sugar

1 egg yolk, lightly beaten

2 tsp vanilla extract

225 g/8 oz plain flour

1 tsp ground cinnamon

Pinch of salt

70 g/2½ oz dried blueberries

70 g/2½ oz dried cranberries

70 g/2½ oz pine nuts, chopped

Directions

• Preheat the oven to 190°C/375°F/Gas Mark 5.

• Line several baking trays with baking paper.

• Place the butter and caster sugar in a large bowl and beat together until light and fluffy, then beat in the egg yolk and vanilla extract.

• Sift together the flour, cinnamon and salt into the mixture. Add the blueberries and cranberries and stir until thoroughly combined.

• Spread out the chopped pine nuts in a shallow dish.

• Scoop up tablespoonfuls of the mixture and roll them into balls. Roll the balls in the pine nuts to coat, then place on the baking trays, spaced well apart, and flatten slightly.

• Bake in the preheated oven for 10–15 minutes.

• Leave to cool on the baking trays for 5–10 minutes, then transfer the biscuits to wire racks to cool completely.

Midnight Biscuits

Makes about 25 biscuits

Ingredients

115 g/4 oz butter, softened

200 g/7 oz caster sugar

1 egg, lightly beaten

½ tsp vanilla extract

115 g/4 oz plain flour

30 g/1 oz cocoa powder

½ tsp bicarbonate of soda

Directions

• Preheat the oven to 180°C/350°F/Gas Mark 4.

• Line several baking trays with baking paper.

• Place the butter and caster sugar in a large bowl and beat together until light and fluffy. Add the egg and vanilla extract and mix until smooth. Sift in the flour, cocoa and bicarbonate of soda and beat until well mixed.

• With dampened hands, roll walnut-sized pieces of the mixture into smooth balls. Place on the baking trays, spaced well apart.

• Bake in the preheated oven for 10–12 minutes or until set.

• Leave to cool on the baking trays for 5 minutes, then transfer the biscuits to wire racks to cool completely.

White Chocolate Cookies

Makes about 30 cookies

Ingredients

115 g/4 oz butter, softened

100 g/3½ oz soft light brown sugar

1 egg, lightly beaten

225 g/8 oz self-raising flour

Pinch of salt

125 g/4½ oz white chocolate, broken into pieces

40 g/1½ oz Brazil nuts, chopped

Directions

• Preheat the oven to 190°C/375°F/Gas Mark 5.

• Line several baking trays with baking paper.

• Place the butter and brown sugar in a large bowl and beat together until light and fluffy. Gradually add the egg, beating well.

• Sift the flour and salt into the creamed mixture and blend well. Stir in the white chocolate chunks and chopped nuts.

• Place dessertspoonfuls of the mixture on the baking trays, putting no more than 6 on each tray because the biscuits will spread during cooking.

• Bake in the preheated oven for 10–12 minutes or until just golden brown.

• Transfer the biscuits to wire racks to cool completely.

Chocolate Chip Cookies

Makes about 30 cookies

Ingredients

275 g/9¾ oz plain flour

1 tsp bicarbonate of soda

1 tsp salt

225 g/8 oz butter, softened

175 g/6 oz soft light brown sugar

150 g/5½ oz caster sugar

1 tsp vanilla extract

2 large eggs

350 g/12 oz plain chocolate chips

125 g/4½ oz walnuts, chopped (optional)

Directions

• Preheat the oven to 190°C/375°F/Gas Mark 5.

• Line several baking trays with baking paper.

• Sift the flour, bicarbonate of soda and salt into a small mixing bowl and mix together. Set aside.

• In another bowl, beat the butter, brown sugar, caster sugar and vanilla extract until light and fluffy.

• Add the eggs one at a time, beating thoroughly after each addition. Stir in the flour mixture until combined. Stir in the chocolate chips and nuts if using. Mix the mixture well.

• Place dessertspoonsful of the mixture on the prepared baking trays about 7.5 cm/3 inches apart.

• Bake in the preheated oven for about 10 minutes or until lightly browned around the edges.

• Leave to cool on the baking trays for 2 minutes, then transfer to wire racks to cool completely.

Banana & Chocolate Biscuits

Makes about 20 biscuits

Ingredients

115 g/4 oz butter, softened

115 g/4 oz caster sugar

1 large egg

1 ripe banana, mashed

1 tsp mixed spice

150 g/5½ oz self-raising flour

2 tbsp milk

55 g/2 oz chocolate chips

55 g/2 oz sultanas or raisins

Directions

- Preheat the oven to 190°C/375°F/Gas Mark 5.

- Line several baking trays with baking paper.

- Place the butter and caster sugar in a bowl and beat together until light and fluffy. Gradually add the egg, beating well after each addition.

- Add the mashed banana to the mixture, beating well.

- Sift the spice and flour together into the mixture and fold in with a palette knife. Add the milk and then fold in the chocolate chips and sultanas.

- Place dessertspoonsful of the mixture on the prepared baking trays about 7.5 cm/3 inches apart.

- Bake in the preheated oven for about 15 minutes or until lightly browned around the edges.

- Leave to cool on the baking trays for 2 minutes, then transfer to wire racks to cool completely.

Chequerboard Biscuits

Makes about 20 biscuits

Ingredients

225 g/8 oz butter, softened

150 g/5½ oz caster sugar

1 egg yolk

2 tsp vanilla extract

225 g/8 oz plain flour

Pinch of salt

1 tsp ground ginger

1 tbsp finely grated orange rind

1 tbsp cocoa powder

1 egg white

Directions

- Preheat the oven to 190°C/375°F/Gas Mark 5.

- Line several baking trays with baking paper.

- Place the butter and caster sugar in a large bowl and beat together until light and fluffy. Add the egg yolk and vanilla extract and mix until smooth. Sift in the flour and salt and stir until combined.

- Divide the mixture in half. Add the ginger and orange rind to one half and mix well. Shape the mixture into a sausage shape, about 15 cm/6 inches long. Flatten the sides and top to make a square. Wrap in clingfilm and chill for 30 minutes.

- Sift the cocoa into the other half of the mixture and mix well. Shape as described for the previous mixture. Wrap in clingfilm and chill for 30 minutes.

- Unwrap both mixtures and cut each lengthways into 3 slices. Cut each slice lengthways into 3 strips. Brush the strips with egg white and stack them in threes, alternating the colours, until they are the same shape as the original shapes. Wrap and chill for 30 minutes.

- Unwrap and slice the mixture. Bake in the preheated oven for 10–12 minutes, or until set.

- Leave to cool on the baking trays for 5 minutes, then transfer the biscuits to wire racks to cool completely.

Mixed Fruit Biscuits

Makes about 26 biscuits

Ingredients

225 g/8 oz butter, softened

150 g/5½ oz caster sugar

1 egg yolk

300 g/10½ oz plain flour

½ tsp ground mixed spice

30 g/1 oz ready-to-eat dried apples, chopped

30 g/1 oz ready-to-eat dried apricots, chopped

55 g/2 oz ready-to-eat dried prunes, chopped

Finely grated rind of 1 orange

Pinch of salt

Directions

• Preheat the oven to 190°C/375°F/Gas Mark 5.

• Line several baking trays with baking paper.

• Place the butter and caster sugar in a large bowl and beat together until light and fluffy. Add the egg yolk and and beat until smooth. Sift in the flour, mixed spice and salt, and stir until combined.

• Add all the dried fruits and the orange rind and mix until thoroughly combined. Shape the mixture into a sausage and wrap in clingfilm and chill for 30 minutes.

• Unwrap the mixture and cut into slices. Put them on the prepared baking trays, spaced well apart.

• Bake in the preheated oven for 10–12 minutes or until golden on the edges.

• Leave to cool on the baking trays for 5 minutes, then transfer the biscuits to wire racks to cool completely.

Muffins

Lemon Poppy Seed Muffins

Makes 12 muffins

Ingredients

225 g/8 oz plain flour

½ tsp salt

1½ tsp baking powder

¼ tsp bicarbonate of soda

115 g/4 oz unsalted butter, softened,
   plus extra for greasing

200 g/7 oz caster sugar

Finely grated rind of 2 lemons

2 large eggs

2 tbsp lemon juice

225 g/8 oz soured cream or crème fraîche

2 tbsp poppy seeds

Glaze

1 tbsp lemon juice

3 tbsp icing sugar

Directions

• Preheat the oven to 180°C/350°F/Gas Mark 4.

• Grease a 12-hole muffin tin or line with 12 paper cases.

• Sift the flour, salt, baking powder and bicarbonate of soda together in a bowl and set aside.

• In a mixing bowl, beat the butter, caster sugar and lemon rind together, until light and creamy. Beat in the eggs one at a time, mixing thoroughly. Stir in a third of the flour mixture until just combined. Stir in the lemon juice and half of the soured cream until combined.

• Fold in half of the remaining flour mixture, and stir until combined. Stir in the remaining soured cream. Finally stir in the remaining flour and the poppy seeds.

• Spoon the mixture into the prepared muffin tin. Bake in the preheated for 20–25 minutes or until golden brown and a cocktail stick or skewer inserted in the centre comes out clean.

• While the muffins are baking make the glaze. Mix the lemon juice and icing sugar together to form a thin glaze.

• Remove the muffins from the oven and leave to cool for 5 minutes. Brush the lemon glaze evenly over the top of each muffin. When cool enough to handle, remove the muffins from the tin and cool completely on a wire rack before serving.

Blueberry Muffins Supreme

Makes 12 muffins

Ingredients

375 g/13 oz plain flour

¾ tsp salt

1 tbsp baking powder

½ tsp bicarbonate of soda

200 g/7 oz caster sugar

115 g/4 oz butter, softened, plus extra
   for greasing

Finely grated rind of 1 lemon

2 tbsp vegetable oil

2 large eggs

225 g/8 oz soured cream or crème fraîche

125 ml/4 fl oz milk

½ tsp lemon extract (optional)

300 g/10½ oz fresh blueberries

Directions

• Preheat the oven to 190°C/375°F/Gas Mark 5.

• Grease a 12-hole muffin tin or line with 12 paper cases.

• Sift the flour, salt, baking powder and bicarbonate of soda together into a bowl. Set aside.

• In a large mixing bowl, beat the caster sugar, butter, lemon rind and vegetable oil until light and creamy. Beat in the eggs one at a time. Whisk in the soured cream, milk and lemon extract.

• Add half the flour mixture and stir until combined. Fold in the rest of the flour and mix thoroughly.

• Fold in the blueberries with a palette knife until just combined.

• Spoon the mixture into the prepared muffin tin. Bake in the preheated oven for 25–30 minutes until golden brown.

• Leave the muffins to cool for 5 minutes, then transfer to a wire rack and leave to cool completely.

Double Chocolate Chip Muffins

Makes 8 muffins

Ingredients

100 g/3½ oz self-raising flour

40 g/1½ oz cocoa powder

115 g/4 oz butter, softened, plus extra
  for greasing

100 g/3½ oz caster sugar

2 large eggs

85 g/3 oz plain chocolate chips

Directions

• Preheat the oven to 190°C/375°F/Gas Mark 5.

• Grease 8 holes in a muffin tin or line with 8 paper
  cases.

• Sift the flour and cocoa powder together in a bowl
  and set aside.

• Beat the butter, caster sugar and eggs together in a
  large mixing bowl until smooth.

• Add half the dry ingredients and stir until combined.
  Add the remaining dry ingredients. Fold in the
  chocolate chips until combined.

• Spoon the mixture into the prepared muffin tin.

• Bake in the preheated oven for 20–25 minutes
  or until well risen and springy to the touch.

• Leave the muffins in the tin to cool for 5 minutes, then
  transfer to a wire rack and leave to cool completely.

Orange & Cranberry Muffins

Makes 12 muffins

Ingredients

225 g/8 oz dried cranberries

3 tbsp fresh orange juice

225 g/8 oz plain flour

1 tbsp baking powder

Pinch of salt

100 g/3½ oz caster sugar

2 large eggs

225 ml/8 fl oz milk

6 tbsp vegetable oil, plus extra for greasing

Finely grated rind of 1 orange

Directions

• Preheat the oven to 200°C/400°F/Gas Mark 6.

• Grease a 12-hole muffin tin or line with 12 paper cases.

• Put the cranberries in a bowl, add the orange juice and leave to soak for 1 hour.

• Sift the flour, baking powder and salt together into a large bowl. Stir in the caster sugar.

• Lightly beat the eggs in a large bowl, then beat in the milk, oil and orange rind. Make a well in the centre of the dry ingredients, pour in the beaten liquid ingredients and add the soaked cranberries and juice. Stir gently until just combined; do not over-mix.

• Spoon the mixture into the prepared muffin tin. Bake in the preheated oven for about 20 minutes until well risen, golden brown and firm to the touch.

• Leave the muffins to cool in the tin for 5 minutes, then serve warm or transfer to a wire rack and leave to cool completely.

Chocolate Marshmallow Muffins

Makes 12 muffins

Ingredients

55 g/2 oz mini white marshmallows

175 g/6 oz plain flour

40 g/1½ oz cocoa powder

1 tbsp baking powder

Pinch of salt

115 g/4 oz soft light brown sugar

2 large eggs

225 ml/8 fl oz milk

6 tbsp vegetable oil, plus extra for greasing

Directions

• Preheat the oven to 200°C/400°F/Gas Mark 6.

• Grease a 12-hole muffin tin or line with 12 paper cases.

• Using scissors, cut the marshmallows in half.

• Sift the flour, cocoa, baking powder and salt together into a large bowl. Stir in the brown sugar and the halved marshmallows.

• Lightly beat the eggs in a large bowl, then beat in the milk and oil.

• Make a well in the centre of the dry ingredients and pour in the beaten liquid ingredients. Stir gently until just combined. Do not over-mix.

• Spoon the mixture into the prepared muffin tin. Bake in the preheated oven for about 20 minutes until well risen and firm to the touch.

• Leave the muffins to cool in the tin for 5 minutes, then serve warm or transfer to a wire rack and leave to cool completely.

Jam Doughnut Muffins

Makes 12 muffins

Ingredients

225 g/8 oz plain flour

1 tbsp baking powder

Pinch of salt

100 g/3½ oz caster sugar

2 large eggs

225 ml/8 fl oz milk

6 tbsp vegetable oil, plus extra for greasing

1 tsp vanilla extract

4 tbsp strawberry or raspberry jam

Topping

115 g/4 oz butter

150 g/5½ oz caster sugar

Directions

• Preheat the oven to 200°C/400°F/Gas Mark 6.

• Grease a 12-hole muffin tin or line with 12 paper cases.

• Sift the flour, baking powder and salt together into a large bowl. Stir in the caster sugar.

• Lightly beat the eggs in a large bowl, then beat in the milk, oil and vanilla extract. Make a well in the centre of the dry ingredients and pour in the beaten liquid ingredients. Stir gently until combined.

• Spoon half the mixture into the prepared muffin tin. Add a teaspoon of jam to the centre of each then spoon in the remaining mixture.

• Bake in the preheated oven for about 20 minutes, until well risen, golden brown and firm to the touch.

• To make the topping, melt the butter. Spread the sugar in a wide shallow bowl. When the muffins are baked, leave them to cool for 5 minutes. Dip the tops of the muffins in the melted butter, then roll in the caster sugar.

• Serve warm or transfer to a wire rack and leave to cool completely.

Banana Muffins

Makes 12 muffins

Ingredients

55 g/2 oz raisins

3 tbsp fresh orange juice

115 g/4 oz plain flour

115 g/4 oz self-raising wholemeal flour

1 tbsp baking powder

100 g/3½ oz caster sugar

2 bananas, mashed

125 ml/4 fl oz milk

2 large eggs

6 tbsp vegetable oil, plus extra for greasing

Grated rind of 1 orange

Directions

• Preheat the oven to 200°C/400°F/Gas Mark 6.

• Grease a 12-hole muffin tin or line with 12 paper cases.

• Put the raisins in a bowl, add the orange juice and leave to soak for 1 hour.

• Sift both types of flour and the baking powder together into a large bowl. Stir in the caster sugar.

• In a separate bowl, whisk the mashed bananas and milk together to form a purée.

• Lightly beat the eggs in a large bowl, then beat in the banana and milk mixture, oil, soaked raisins, orange juice and rind. Make a well in the centre of the dry ingredients and pour in the beaten liquid ingredients. Stir gently until just combined; do not over-mix.

• Spoon the mixture into the prepared muffin tin. Bake in the preheated oven for about 20 minutes, until well risen, golden brown and firm to the touch.

• Leave the muffins to cool in the tin for 5 minutes, then serve warm or transfer to a wire rack and let cool completely.

Carrot Cake Muffins

Makes 12 muffins

Ingredients

225 g/8 oz plain flour

1 tbsp baking powder

Pinch of salt

1 tsp mixed spice

115 g/4 oz soft light brown sugar

115 g/4 oz grated carrots

55 g/2 oz chopped walnuts or pecan nuts

70 g/2½ oz sultanas

2 large eggs

175 ml/6 fl oz milk

6 tbsp vegetable oil, plus extra for greasing

Finely grated rind and juice of 1 orange

Strips of orange zest, to decorate

Icing

115 g/4 oz soft cream cheese

40 g/1½ oz butter, softened

50 g/1¾ oz icing sugar

Directions

• Preheat the oven to 200°C/400°F/Gas Mark 6.

• Grease a 12-hole muffin tin or line with 12 paper cases.

• Sift the flour, baking powder, salt and mixed spice together into a large bowl. Stir in the brown sugar, grated carrots, walnuts and sultanas.

• Lightly beat the eggs in a large bowl, then beat in the milk, oil, orange rind and orange juice. Make a well in the centre of the dry ingredients and pour in the beaten liquid ingredients. Stir gently until just combined; do not over-mix.

• Spoon the mixture into the prepared muffin tin. Bake in the preheated oven for about 20 minutes until well risen, golden brown and firm to the touch.

• Leave the muffins to cool for 5 minutes, then transfer to a wire rack and leave to cool completely.

• To make the icing, put the cream cheese and butter in a bowl and sift in the icing sugar. Beat together until light and fluffy. When the muffins are cold, spread the icing on top of each, then decorate with strips of orange zest.

• Chill the muffins in the fridge until ready to serve.

Spiced Apple Muffins

Makes 12 muffins

Ingredients

115 g/4 oz plain flour

1 tbsp baking powder

1 tsp mixed spice

115 g/4 oz soft light brown sugar

175 g/6 oz porridge oats

2 large cooking apples

2 large eggs

125 ml/4 fl oz milk

100 ml/3½ fl oz unsweetened apple juice

6 tbsp vegetable oil, plus extra for greasing

Directions

- Preheat the oven to 200°C/400°F/Gas Mark 6.

- Grease a 12-hole muffin tin or line with 12 paper cases.

- Sift the flour, baking powder and mixed spice together into a large bowl. Stir in the brown sugar and 85 g/3 oz of the oats.

- Finely chop the unpeeled apples, discarding the cores. Add to the flour mixture and stir together.

- Lightly beat the eggs in a large bowl, then beat in the milk, apple juice and oil. Make a well in the centre of the dry ingredients and pour in the beaten liquid ingredients. Stir gently until just combined; do not over-mix.

- Spoon the mixture into the prepared muffin tin. Sprinkle the tops of the muffins with the remaining oats. Bake in the preheated oven for about 20 minutes until well risen, golden brown and firm to the touch.

- Leave the muffins to cool in the tin for 5 minutes, then serve warm or transfer to a wire rack and leave to cool completely.

Iced Cream Cheese Muffins

Makes 12 muffins

Ingredients

115 g/4 oz soft cream cheese

100 g/3½ oz caster sugar

225 g/8 oz plain flour

1 tbsp baking powder

Pinch of salt

115 g/4 oz soft light brown sugar

2 large eggs

225 g/8 oz soured cream or crème fraîche

6 tbsp vegetable oil, plus extra for greasing

Finely grated rind of 1 lemon

Icing

115 g/4 oz soft cream cheese

50 g/1¾ oz icing sugar

2 tsp fresh lemon juice

Directions

• Preheat the oven to 200°C/400°F/Gas Mark 6.

• Grease a 12-hole muffin tin or line with 12 paper cases.

• Put the cream cheese in a bowl. Sift in the caster sugar and beat together.

• Sift the flour, baking powder and salt together into a large bowl. Stir in the brown sugar.

• Lightly beat the eggs in a large bowl, then beat in the soured cream, oil and lemon rind. Make a well in the centre of the dry ingredients and pour in the liquid ingredients. Stir gently until combined, do not over-mix.

• Spoon half the mixture into the prepared muffin tin. Add a spoonful of the cream cheese mixture to the centre of each, then spoon in the remaining mixture. Bake in the preheated oven for about 20 minutes until well risen, golden brown and firm to the touch.

• Leave the muffins to cool for 5 minutes, then transfer to a wire rack and leave to cool completely.

• To make the icing, put the cream cheese in a bowl and sift in the icing sugar. Add the lemon juice and beat well together. Spread the icing on top of the muffins. Chill in the fridge until ready to serve.

Raspberry Crumble Muffins

Makes 12 muffins

Ingredients

225 g/8 oz plain flour

1 tbsp baking powder

½ tsp bicarbonate of soda

Pinch of salt

100 g/3½ oz caster sugar

2 large eggs

225 g/8 oz natural yogurt

6 tbsp vegetable oil, plus extra for greasing

1 tsp vanilla extract

250 g/9 oz frozen raspberries, thawed

Topping

60 g/2¼ oz plain flour

40 g/1½ oz butter, softened

25 g/1 oz caster sugar

Directions

- Preheat the oven to 200°C/400°F/Gas Mark 6.

- Grease a 12-hole muffin tin or line with 12 paper cases.

- To make the topping, put the flour into a bowl. Cut the butter into small pieces, add to the bowl with the flour and rub it in with your fingertips until the mixture resembles fine breadcrumbs. Stir in the caster sugar and set aside.

- To make the muffins, sift the flour, baking powder, bicarbonate of soda and salt together into a large bowl. Stir in the caster sugar.

- Lightly beat the eggs in a large bowl, then beat in the yogurt, oil and vanilla extract. Make a well in the centre of the dry ingredients, pour in the beaten liquid ingredients and add the raspberries. Stir gently until just combined, do not over-mix.

- Spoon the mixture into the prepared muffin tin. Scatter the crumble topping over each muffin and press down lightly. Bake in the preheated oven for about 20 minutes until well risen, golden brown and firm to the touch.

- Leave the muffins to cool in the tin for 5 minutes, then serve warm or transfer to a wire rack and leave to cool completely.

Soured Cream Muffins

Makes 12 muffins

Ingredients

225 g/8 oz plain flour

Pinch of salt

1 tbsp baking powder

100 g/3½ oz caster sugar

2 large eggs

225 g/8 oz soured cream or crème fraîche

6 tbsp vegetable oil, plus extra for greasing

1 tsp vanilla extract

Directions

- Preheat the oven to 190°C/375°F/Gas Mark 5.

- Grease a 12-hole muffin tin or line with 12 paper cases.

- Sift the flour, salt, baking powder and caster sugar together into a bowl. Set aside.

- Lightly beat the eggs in a large mixing bowl, then beat in the soured cream, oil and vanilla extract.

- Add half the flour mixture and stir until combined. Fold in the rest of the flour and mix thoroughly.

- Spoon the mixture into the prepared muffin tin. Bake in the preheated oven for 20–25 minutes until golden brown.

- Leave the muffins to cool in the tin for 5 minutes, then transfer to a wire rack and leave to cool completely.

Doughnuts & Pastries

Simple Doughnuts

Makes 10–12 doughnuts

Ingredients

175ml/6 fl oz milk

40 g/1½ oz butter

300 g/10½ oz strong white flour, plus

    extra for dusting

¼ tsp salt

1½ tsp easy-blend dried yeast

25 g/1 oz caster sugar

1 large egg, beaten

Vegetable oil, for oiling and deep-frying

Glaze

115 g/4 oz icing sugar

2-3 tbsp milk

Directions

• Place the milk and butter in a small saucepan and heat gently until the butter has melted. Cool for 5 minutes.

• Sift the flour into a large bowl and stir in the salt, yeast and sugar. Pour in the milk mixture and the egg and mix to a soft dough. Turn onto a floured surface and knead for 5-6 minutes until smooth and elastic, adding a little more flour if needed.

• Place the dough in a bowl, cover and leave in a warm place for 1- 1½ hours or until almost doubled in size. Line a large baking sheet with baking paper.

• Knock the dough back and roll out on a lightly floured surface to a 1½-cm/⅝-inch thickness. Using a 9-cm/3½-inch doughnut cutter, stamp out 7 doughnuts. Lightly re-

knead the trimmings, roll out and stamp out another 3 doughnuts. Place on the baking sheet. Cover with lightly oiled clingfilm and leave in a warm place for 10 minutes until puffy.

• Half-fill a large deep pan with oil and heat to 180°C/350°F, or until a cube of bread browns in 30 seconds. Fry the doughnuts, 2-3 at a time, for 1-2 minutes on each side, or until golden. Remove with a slotted spoon and drain thoroughly on kitchen paper. Place on a wire rack set over a baking sheet.

• To make the glaze, sift the icing sugar into a bowl and gradually beat in the milk to make a smooth icing. Spoon the icing over the warm doughnuts, allowing the excess to run off. Leave the iced doughnuts to cool completely.

Double Chocolate Swirls

Makes 24 swirls

Ingredients

550 g/1lb 4 oz strong white flour, plus
    extra for dusting

7 g/¼ oz easy-blend dried yeast

100 g/3½ oz caster sugar

½ tsp salt

1 tsp ground cinnamon

85 g/3 oz butter, softened, plus extra
    for greasing

2 large eggs, beaten

300 ml/10 fl oz milk

Filling and Glaze

6 tbsp chocolate hazelnut spread

175 g/6 oz milk chocolate, chopped

1 egg, beaten

Directions

• Lightly grease two baking trays.

• Mix the flour, yeast, caster sugar, salt and cinnamon
  together in a large bowl.

• Melt the butter in a heatproof bowl set over a saucepan
  of gently simmering water, then leave to cool slightly.
  Whisk in the eggs and milk. Pour into the flour mixture
  and mix well to form a dough.

• Turn out on to a floured surface and knead for
  10 minutes, until smooth. Put into a large floured
  bowl, cover with clingfilm and put in a warm place
  for 1½–2 hours until doubled in bulk.

• Preheat the oven to 220°C/425°F/Gas Mark 7.

• Remove the mixture from the bowl and knock back.

• Divide the mixture into four pieces and roll each piece
  into a rectangle about 2.5 cm/1 inch thick. Spread each
  rectangle with the chocolate hazelnut spread and
  scatter with the chopped chocolate.

• Roll up each rectangle from one of the long edges,
  then cut into six pieces. Place each swirl, cut-side
  down, on the prepared baking trays and brush well
  with the beaten egg. Bake in the preheated oven for
  12–15 minutes and serve warm.

Jam Doughnuts

Makes 10 doughnuts

Ingredients

400 g/14 oz strong white flour, plus extra
  for dusting

55 g/2 oz butter, cut into pieces

2 tbsp caster sugar, plus extra for dusting

$\frac{1}{2}$ tsp salt

7 g/$\frac{1}{4}$ oz easy-blend dried yeast

1 egg, lightly beaten

175 ml/6 fl oz lukewarm milk

Vegetable oil, for greasing and frying

Filling

150 g/5$\frac{1}{2}$ oz strawberry or raspberry jam

Directions

• Lightly grease a large bowl and 2 baking trays.

• Place the flour in a large bowl, add the butter and rub it in until the mixture resembles breadcrumbs. Stir in the caster sugar, salt and yeast. Make a well in the centre and add the egg and milk, then mix to form a soft, pliable mixture. Knead well for 10 minutes.

• Place in the greased bowl and cover. Leave in a warm place to rise for about 1 hour or until doubled in bulk.

• Knead the mixture on a floured work surface, then divide into 10 pieces. Shape each piece into a ball and place on the baking trays. Cover and leave in a warm place to double in size for 45 minutes.

• Heat 7.5–10 cm/3–4 inches of oil in a saucepan to 180–190°C/350–375°F or until a cube of bread browns in 30 seconds. Deep-fry the doughnuts in batches for 2–3 minutes on each side. Drain on kitchen paper and dust with sugar.

• To fill the doughnuts, place the jam in a piping bag fitted with a plain nozzle. Insert a sharp knife into each doughnut and twist to make a hole. Push the point of the nozzle into the hole and pipe in some jam.

Cream & Jam Turnovers

Makes 8 turnovers

Pastry

450 g/1 lb puff pastry, thawed if frozen

Plain flour for dusting

1 egg, for glazing

1 tbsp water

Filling

4 tbsp caster sugar

225 ml/8 fl oz double cream

1 tsp vanilla extract

4 tbsp raspberry or strawberry jam

Directions

• Preheat the oven to 220°C/425°F/Gas Mark 7.

• Line a large baking tray with baking paper.

• Roll the pastry out on a lightly floured work surface to a little larger than 25 cm/10 inches square. Using a sharp knife, trim the edges and cut out 4 x 13-cm/5-inch squares. Cut each square in half diagonally to produce 8 triangles and place on the lined baking tray.

• Beat the egg with the water and brush over the tops of the triangles, taking care not to let it run down the sides. Sprinkle the tops with half the caster sugar.

• Bake in the preheated oven for 15 minutes or until risen, crisp and golden. Transfer to a wire rack to cool completely.

• Place the cream, remaining sugar and vanilla extract in a large bowl and whip until soft peaks form. Spoon into a piping bag fitted with a star nozzle. Split the puff pastry triangles in half horizontally and spread jam on the bases.

• Pipe the cream on top of the jam and sandwich the 2 halves back together. Chill in the fridge until required.

Cream Éclairs

Makes 6–8 éclairs

Choux Pastry

150 ml/5 fl oz water

70 g/2½ oz butter, cut into pieces

100 g/3½ oz plain flour, sifted

2 eggs, beaten

Pastry Cream

2 eggs, lightly beaten

55 g/2 oz caster sugar

2 tbsp cornflour

300 ml/10 fl oz milk

¼ tsp vanilla extract

450 ml/16 fl oz whipping cream, whipped

Icing

25 g/1 oz butter

1 tbsp milk

1 tbsp cocoa powder

60 g/2¼ oz icing sugar

40 g/1½ oz white chocolate, broken into pieces

Directions

• Preheat the oven to 200°C/400°F/Gas Mark 6 and lightly grease a baking tray. Sprinkle the baking tray with water.

• To make the pastry, place the water in a saucepan, add the butter and heat gently until the butter melts. Bring to a rolling boil, then remove the pan from the heat and add the flour all at once, beating well until the mixture leaves the sides of the pan and forms a ball. Leave to cool slightly, then gradually beat in the eggs to form a smooth, glossy mixture. Spoon into a large piping bag fitted with a 1-cm/½-inch plain nozzle.

• Pipe éclairs 7.5 cm/3 inches long, spaced apart, on the prepared baking tray. Bake in the oven for 30–35 minutes until crisp and golden. Make a small slit in the side of each éclair to let the steam escape. Cool on a wire rack.

• Meanwhile, make the pastry cream. Whisk the eggs and caster sugar until thick and creamy. Fold in the cornflour. Heat the milk in a saucepan until almost boiling and pour on to the egg mixture, whisking. Transfer the egg mixture to the saucepan and cook over a low heat, stirring until thick. Remove the pan from the heat and stir in the vanilla extract. Cover with baking paper and leave cool. Once cool, fold in the whipped cream.

• To make the icing, melt the butter with the milk in a saucepan, remove from the heat and stir in the cocoa and icing sugar. Split the éclairs lengthways and pipe in the pastry cream. Spread the icing over the top of the éclairs. Melt the white chocolate in a heatproof bowl set over a saucepan of simmering water, then drizzle over the chocolate icing and leave to set.

Soured Cream Doughnuts

Makes 24 doughnuts

Ingredients

200 g/7 oz caster sugar

3 eggs

225 g/8 oz soured cream or crème fraîche

1 tsp vanilla extract

2 tbsp vegetable oil

450 g/1 lb plain flour, plus extra for dusting

1 tsp bicarbonate of soda

1 tsp baking powder

½ tsp salt

¼ tsp nutmeg

Vegetable oil, for frying

Glaze

175 g/6 oz icing sugar

3–4 tbsp water (or milk)

Directions

• Beat sugar and eggs thoroughly in a large bowl. Add the soured cream, vanilla extract and oil. Mix well.

• Add the dry ingredients and mix well again. Turn out on to a floured board and knead for 5 minutes. The mixture should be fairly soft.

• Roll out the mixture to a 5 mm/¼ inch thickness. Cut out 24 rounds with a floured doughnut cutter.

• Heat 7.5 cm/3 inches of vegetable oil in a saucepan to 180°–190°C/350–375°F, or until a cube of bread browns in 30 seconds. Cook the doughnuts in batches by dropping them into the hot oil. Fry for 2 minutes on each side or until golden brown.

• Remove with a slotted spoon and drain on kitchen paper or wire rack. Leave to cool.

• To make the glaze, place the sugar in a bowl and slowly mix in the water or milk until smooth.

• Pour the glaze over the cooled doughnuts.

Cinnamon Swirl Rolls

Makes 8 rolls

Ingredients

350 g/12 oz self-raising flour, plus extra for dusting

Pinch of salt

2 tbsp caster sugar

1 tsp ground cinnamon

115 g/4 oz butter, melted, plus extra for greasing

2 egg yolks

225 ml/8 fl oz milk, plus extra for glazing

Filling

1 tsp ground cinnamon

55 g/2 oz soft light brown sugar

2 tbsp caster sugar

1 tbsp butter, melted

Icing

115 g/4 oz icing sugar

2 tbsp cream cheese, softened

1 tbsp butter, softened

2 tbsp boiling water, plus extra if needed

1 tsp vanilla extract

Directions

• Preheat the oven to 180°C/350°F/Gas Mark 4.

• Grease a round baking tin and line the base with baking paper.

• Mix the flour, salt, sugar and cinnamon together in a bowl. Whisk the butter, egg yolks and milk together and combine with the dry ingredients to make a soft mixture. Turn out on to a large piece of greaseproof paper lightly sprinkled with flour, and roll out to a rectangle measuring 30 x 25 cm/12 x 10 inches.

• To make the filling, mix the ingredients together, spread evenly over the dough and roll up to form a sausage shape. Using a sharp knife, cut the dough into 8 even-sized slices and pack into the prepared tin.

• Brush gently with milk and bake in the preheated oven for 30–35 minutes or until golden brown. Remove from the oven and leave to cool for 5 minutes before removing from the tin.

• To make the icing, sift the icing sugar into a large bowl and make a well in the centre. Place the cream cheese and butter in the centre, pour over the boiling water and stir to mix. Add extra water, a few drops at a time, until the icing coats the back of a spoon. Stir in the vanilla extract.

• Drizzle the icing over the rolls. Serve warm or cooled.

Chocolate Cake Doughnuts

Makes 10–14 doughnuts

Ingredients

125 ml/4 fl oz milk, warmed

1 egg

1 tsp vanilla extract

30 g/1 oz cocoa powder

225 g/8 oz plain flour, plus extra for dusting

½ tsp bicarbonate of soda

½ tsp baking powder

½ tsp salt

100 g/3½ oz caster sugar

25 g/1 oz butter

Vegetable oil, for greasing and frying

Glaze

50 g/1¾ oz plain chocolate, broken into pieces

50 g/1¾ oz white chocolate, broken into pieces

Directions

• Blend together the warmed milk, egg and vanilla extract in a bowl.

• In a mixer with a paddle attachment, mix together the cocoa powder, flour, bicarbonate of soda, baking powder, salt and sugar. Add the butter and blend. Slowly add the milk, egg and vanilla. Mix until the mixture is smooth and thick.

• Leave the mixture to rest in the mixer for 20 minutes.

• Roll the mixture on to a floured surface to about 1-cm/½-inch thick. Using a doughnut cutter, cut out 10–14 rounds.

• Heat at least 7.5 cm/3 inches of vegetable oil in a heavy based saucepan to 180–190°C/350–375°F, or until a cube of bread browns in 30 seconds. Carefully place the doughnuts a few at a time into the oil. Fry for 2 minutes on each side or until golden brown. Remove with a slotted spoon and drain on a wire rack.

• To make the glaze, melt each of the chocolates separately in heatproof bowls over saucepans of simmering water. Decorate the doughnuts with the melted chocolates, making a pattern.

Strawberry Profiteroles

Makes 12 profiteroles

Choux Pastry

100 g/3½ oz plain flour

2 tbsp cocoa powder

Pinch of salt

85 g/3 oz butter

225 ml/8 fl oz water

2 eggs, plus 1 egg white, beaten

Filling and Topping

2 tsp powdered gelatine

2 tbsp water

500 g/1 lb 2 oz strawberries, hulled

225 g/8 oz ricotta cheese

1 tbsp caster sugar

2 tsp strawberry-flavoured liqueur
(optional)

Icing sugar, for dusting

Directions

• To make the filling, sprinkle the gelatine over the water in a heatproof bowl. Leave it to soften for 2–3 minutes. Place the bowl over a saucepan of gently simmering water and stir until the gelatine dissolves. Remove from the heat. Place 175 g/6 oz of the strawberries in a blender with the ricotta cheese, sugar and liqueur. Process until blended. Add the gelatine and process briefly. Transfer the mousse to a bowl, cover with clingfilm and chill for 1–1½ hours, until set.

• Preheat the oven to 220°C/425°F/Gas Mark 7. Line a baking tray with baking paper. To make the pastry, sift the flour, cocoa and salt together into a bowl. Put the butter and water into a heavy-based saucepan and heat gently until the butter has melted. Bring to a rolling boil, then remove the pan from the heat and add the flour,

cocoa, and salt, beating well until the mixture leaves the sides of the pan. Leave to cool slightly.

• Gradually beat the eggs and egg white into the flour mixture and continue beating until it is smooth and glossy. Drop 12 dessert spoonfuls of the mixture on to the baking tray and bake in the preheated oven for 20–25 minutes until puffed up and crisp. Make a slit in the side of each pastry puff. Return to the oven for 5 minutes. Remove from the oven and cool on a wire rack.

• Slice the remaining strawberries. Cut the choux pastries in half, divide the mousse and strawberry slices between them, then replace the tops. Dust with icing sugar and place in the fridge. Serve within 1½ hours.

Spiced Doughnut Holes

Makes 18–20 holes

Ingredients

125 ml/4 fl oz milk, warmed

1 egg

2 tbsp natural yogurt

1 tsp vanilla extract

225 g/8 oz plain flour

2 tsp baking powder

½ tsp salt

70 g/2½ oz caster sugar

1 tsp grated nutmeg

25 g/1 oz butter

Vegetable oil, for greasing and frying

icing sugar, for dusting

Directions

• Mix the warm milk, egg, yogurt and vanilla extract together in a bowl.

• In a mixer with a paddle attachment, mix the flour, baking powder, salt, sugar and nutmeg. Slowly add the butter and blend. Slowly add the milk mixture until the mixture is smooth and thick.

• Leave the dough to rest in the mixer for 20 minutes.

• Heat at least 7.5 cm/3 inches vegetable oil in a heavy-based saucepan to 180–190°C/350–375°F, or until a cube of bread browns in 30 seconds.

• Drop the mixture, 1 tablespoonful at a time, into the oil. Fry, in batches, for a minute or until golden brown. Remove and drain on a kitchen paper or wire rack.

• Sprinkle with icing sugar and serve.

Everyday Cakes

Lemon Loaf Cake

Serves 8–10

Ingredients

175 g/6 oz plain flour

1 tsp baking powder

175 g/6 oz butter, softened, plus extra
  for greasing

150 g/5½ oz caster sugar

3 eggs, beaten

1 egg yolk

Finely grated rind of 1 lemon

2 tbsp lemon juice

Fine strips of lemon zest, to decorate

Syrup

100 g/3½ oz icing sugar

3 tbsp lemon juice

Directions

- Preheat the oven to 180°C/350°F/Gas Mark 4.

- Grease a 23 x 13 x 7.5-cm/9 x 5 x 3-inch loaf tin and line with baking paper.

- Sift the flour and baking powder into a large bowl and add the butter, caster sugar, eggs and egg yolk. Beat well until the mixture is smooth, then stir in the lemon rind and juice.

- Spoon the mixture into the prepared tin and smooth the surface with a palette knife. Bake in the preheated oven for 40–50 minutes or until well risen and golden brown.

- Remove the tin from the oven and transfer to a wire rack.

- For the syrup, put the icing sugar and lemon juice into a saucepan and heat gently without boiling, stirring, until the sugar dissolves.

- Prick the top of the hot cake several times with a skewer or cocktail stick and spoon the syrup over it. Leave to cool completely in the tin, then turn out, sprinkle with strips of lemon zest and serve in slices.

Loaf Cake with Orange Glaze

Serves 8–10

Ingredients

250 g/9 oz plain flour

1 tsp baking powder

¼ tsp bicarbonate of soda

½ tsp salt

225 g/8 oz unsalted butter, plus
   extra for greasing

250 g/9 oz caster sugar

1 tbsp grated lemon rind

1 tbsp grated orange rind

4 eggs

1 tsp vanilla extract

125 ml/4 fl oz buttermilk

Glaze

115 g/4 oz icing sugar

1½ tbsp fresh orange juice

1 tbsp grated orange rind

Directions

• Preheat the oven to 160°C/325°F/Gas Mark 3.

• Grease a 23 x 13 x 7.5-cm/9 x 5 x 3-inch loaf tin and
line with baking paper.

• Sift the flour, baking powder, bicarbonate of soda and
salt together in a mixing bowl.

• Using an electric mixer, beat the butter, caster sugar
and rinds until light and creamy in a large mixing bowl.
Beat in the eggs, one at a time, beating very thoroughly
after each addition. Add the vanilla extract.

• Using a palette knife, mix in the flour alternately with
the buttermilk, ending with flour.

• Spoon the mixture into the prepared loaf tin and
smooth the top.

• Bake in the preheated oven for 60 minutes or until a
skewer or cocktail stick inserted in the centre comes
out clean. Remove and leave to rest for 15 minutes,
then turn out on to a wire rack. Leave to cool for
15 minutes before glazing.

• To make the glaze, combine the sugar, orange juice
and rind in a bowl, adding enough orange juice to get
a smooth spreadable consistency. Spread over the top
of the warm cake.

• Leave the cake to cool completely before serving.

Banana Loaf Cake

Serves 8–10

Ingredients

115 g/4 oz white self-raising flour

100 g/3½ oz wholemeal self-raising flour

175 g/6 oz soft light brown sugar

Pinch of salt

½ tsp ground cinnamon

½ tsp ground nutmeg

2 large ripe bananas, mashed

175 ml/6 fl oz orange juice

2 eggs, beaten

4 tbsp vegetable oil, plus extra
   for greasing

Directions

• Preheat the oven to 180°C/350°F/Gas Mark 4.

• Grease a 23 x 13 x 7.5-cm/9 x 5 x 3-inch loaf tin and line with baking paper.

• Sift the flours, brown sugar, salt and the spices into a large bowl. Set aside.

• In a separate bowl, mash the bananas with the orange juice, then beat in the eggs and oil. Pour into the dry ingredients and mix well.

• Spoon the mixture into the prepared loaf tin and bake in the preheated oven for 60 minutes or until a skewer or cocktail stick inserted into the centre comes out clean.

• Remove from the oven and leave to cool in the tin. Turn out the cake, slice and serve.

Banana & Cranberry Loaf Cake

Serves 8–10

Ingredients

175 g/6 oz self-raising flour

½ tsp baking powder

225 g/8 oz soft light brown sugar

2 bananas, mashed

40 g/1½ oz mixed peel, chopped

40 g/1½ oz mixed nuts, chopped

50 g/1¾ oz dried cranberries

5–6 tbsp orange juice

2 eggs, beaten

150 ml/5 fl oz vegetable oil, plus
   extra for greasing

Icing

70 g/2½ oz icing sugar, sifted

2 tsp water

Grated rind of 1 orange

Directions

• Preheat the oven to 180°C/350°F/Gas Mark 4.

• Grease a 23 x 13 x 7.5-cm/9 x 5 x 3-inch loaf tin and line with baking paper.

• Sift the flour and baking powder into a large mixing bowl. Stir in the brown sugar, bananas, mixed peel, nuts and cranberries.

• Stir the orange juice, eggs and oil together until well combined, then add the mixture to the dry ingredients and mix until well blended. Pour into the prepared tin.

• Bake in the preheated oven for about 60 minutes until firm to the touch and a skewer or cocktail stick inserted into the centre comes out clean.

• Turn out on to a wire rack and leave to cool.

• Mix the icing sugar with a little water and drizzle the icing over the cake. Sprinkle the orange rind over the top. Leave the icing to set before slicing.

Blackberry & Apple Loaf Cake

Serves 8–10

Ingredients

2 large eating apples

3 tbsp lemon juice

300 g/10½ oz self-raising wholemeal flour

½ tsp baking powder

1 tsp ground cinnamon

70 g/2½ oz blackberries, thawed, if frozen

175 g/6 oz soft light brown sugar

1 egg, beaten

225 g/8 oz natural yogurt

butter or oil for greasing

Topping

35 g/1¼ oz blackberries, thawed, if frozen

14 white or brown sugar lumps, crushed

Directions

• Preheat the oven to 190°C/375°F/Gas Mark 5.

• Grease a 23 x 13 x 7.5-cm/9 x 5 x 3-inch loaf tin and line with baking paper.

• Peel, core and finely dice the apples. Place them in a saucepan with the lemon juice, bring to the boil, cover and simmer for about 10 minutes until soft and pulpy. Beat well and set aside to cool.

• Sift the flour, baking powder and cinnamon into a bowl. Stir in the blackberries and the brown sugar.

• Make a well in the centre of the ingredients and add the egg, yogurt and cooled apple purée. Mix well to incorporate thoroughly.

• Spoon the mixture into the prepared tin and smooth the top. Sprinkle with the remaining blackberries, pressing them down into the cake mixture and top with the crushed sugar lumps. Bake in the preheated oven for 40–45 minutes. Remove from the oven and set aside in the tin to cool.

• Turn out the cake, slice and serve.

Chocolate Chip Loaf Cake

Serves 8–10

Ingredients

150 g/5½ oz butter, softened, plus extra
  for greasing

150 g/5½ oz caster sugar

1 tsp vanilla extract

3 eggs, lightly beaten

175 g/6 oz self-raising flour

85 g/3 oz plain chocolate chips

Glaze

85 g/3 oz plain chocolate, broken into
  pieces

2 tbsp coffee liqueur or strong black coffee

1 tsp vanilla extract

1 tbsp golden syrup

Whipped cream or crème fraiche, to serve
(optional)

Directions

• Preheat the oven to 160°C/325°F/Gas Mark 3.

• Grease a 23 x 13 x 7.5-cm/9 x 5 x 3-inch loaf tin and line with baking paper.

• Place the butter and sugar in a large mixing bowl and using an electric hand-held whisk, beat together until pale and fluffy. Beat in the vanilla extract.

• Gradually add the eggs, beating well after each addition. Sift over the flour and fold in using a metal spoon. Fold in three-quarters of the chocolate chips.

• Spoon the mixture into the prepared tin and gently level the surface with a small palette knife. Scatter over the rest of the chocolate chips.

• Bake in the preheated oven for 50–55 minutes, or until the cake is risen, golden and firm to the touch and a skewer inserted into the centre of the cake comes out clean.

• Leave the cake in the tin for 5–10 minutes, then turn out onto a wire rack and leave to cool completely.

• For the glaze, place the chocolate, coffee liqueur, vanilla extract and golden syrup in a heatproof bowl set over a pan of simmering water and leave until the chocolate has melted. Remove from the heat and stir until smooth and glossy. Cool for 5 minutes.

• Drizzle the warm glaze over the cake and serve with whipped cream or crème fraiche, if liked.

Madeira Loaf Cake

Serves 8–10 per cake

Ingredients

400 g/14 oz plain flour

1 tsp salt

1 tbsp baking powder

450 g/1 lb unsalted butter, plus extra
for greasing

400 g/14 oz caster sugar

1½ tsp vanilla extract

8 large eggs

Directions

• Preheat the oven to 180°C/350°F/Gas Mark 4.

• Grease two 23 x 13 x 7.5-cm/9 x 5 x 3-inch loaf tins and line with baking paper.

• Combine the flour, salt and baking powder in a bowl and set aside.

• In a large bowl, cream the butter and caster sugar with a mixer until pale and fluffy. Add the vanilla extract and mix thoroughly.

• Lightly beat the 8 eggs and add to the butter and sugar, mixing until just incorporated. Fold in the flour mixture. Divide the mixture between the prepared tins.

• Bake in the preheated oven for about 65 minutes until a skewer or cocktail stick inserted into the centre of each cake comes out clean.

• Leave the tins on a wire rack to cool for 30 minutes before removing the cakes from the tins.

Blueberry Soured Cream Loaf Cake

Serves 8–10

Ingredients

150 g/5½ oz butter, softened, plus extra
  for greasing

150 g/5½ oz caster sugar, plus an extra 2 tsp

1 tsp vanilla extract

3 eggs, lightly beaten

3 tbsp soured cream

200 g/7 oz self-raising flour

125 g/4½ oz fresh blueberries

Frosting (optional)

150 ml/5 fl oz double cream

1 tbsp icing sugar, sifted

1 tsp finely grated lemon rind

Directions

• Preheat the oven to 180°C/350°F/Gas Mark 4.

• Grease a 23 x 13 x 7.5-cm/9 x 5 x 3-inch loaf tin and line with baking paper.

• Place the butter and sugar in a large mixing bowl and using an electric hand-held whisk, beat together until pale and fluffy. Beat in the vanilla extract.

• Gradually add the eggs, beating well after each addition. Stir in the soured cream. Sift over the flour and fold into the creamed mixture using a metal spoon. Fold in two thirds of the blueberries.

• Spoon the mixture into the prepared tin, gently level the surface with a small palette knife. Scatter over the rest of the blueberries and sprinkle with the extra 2 teaspoons of caster sugar.

• Bake in the preheated oven for 55 minutes–1 hour, or until the cake is risen, golden and firm to the touch and a skewer inserted into the centre of the cake comes out clean.

• Leave the cake in the tin for 5–10 minutes, then turn out onto a wire rack and leave to cool completely.

• To make the frosting, place the cream and icing sugar in a bowl and whip until holding soft peaks. Fold in the lemon rind. Spread over the top of the cake, if liked, or serve on the side.

Poppy Seed Loaf Cake

Serves 8–10

Ingredients

150 g/5½ oz butter, softened, plus extra
   for greasing

150 g/5½ oz caster sugar

1 tsp finely grated lemon rind

3 eggs, lightly beaten

175 g/6 oz self-raising flour

1½ tsp poppy seeds

Directions

• Preheat the oven to 160°C/325°F/Gas Mark 3.

• Grease a 23 x 13 x 7.5-cm/9 x 5 x 3-inch loaf tin and line with baking paper.

• Place the butter and sugar in a large mixing bowl and using an electric hand-held whisk, beat together until pale and fluffy. Beat in the lemon rind.

• Gradually add the eggs, beating well after each addition. Sift over the flour and fold into the creamed mixture using a metal spoon. Fold in the poppy seeds.

• Spoon the mixture into the prepared tin and gently level the surface with a small palette knife.

• Bake in the preheated oven for 50–55 minutes, or until the cake is risen, golden and firm to the touch and a skewer inserted into the centre of the cake comes out clean.

• Leave the cake in the tin for 5–10 minutes, then turn out onto a wire rack and leave to cool completely.

Date & Walnut Loaf Cake

Serves 8–10

Ingredients

70 g/2½ oz chopped stoned dates

½ tsp bicarbonate of soda

Finely grated rind of ½ lemon

125 ml/4 fl oz hot black tea

40 g/1½ oz butter, plus extra for greasing

70 g/2½ oz soft light brown sugar

1 egg

115 g/4 oz self-raising flour

30 g/1 oz chopped walnuts

Walnut halves, to decorate

Directions

• Preheat the oven to 180°C/350°F/Gas Mark 4.

• Grease a 23 x 13 x 7.5-cm/9 x 5 x 3-inch loaf tin and line with baking paper.

• Place the dates, bicarbonate of soda and lemon rind in a bowl and add the hot tea. Leave to soak for 10 minutes until softened.

• Cream the butter and caster sugar together until light and fluffy, then beat in the egg. Stir in the date mixture.

• Fold in the flour using a large metal spoon, then fold in the chopped walnuts. Spoon the mixture into the prepared loaf tin and spread evenly. Top with walnut halves.

• Bake in the preheated oven for 35–40 minutes or until risen, firm and golden brown. Leave to cool in the tin for 10 minutes, then turn out the cake and finish cooling on a wire rack.

Chocolate Peanut Butter Loaf Cake

Serves 8–10

Ingredients

175 g/6 oz butter, softened, plus extra for
  greasing

175 g/6 oz caster sugar

1 tsp vanilla extract

3 eggs, lightly beaten

175 g/6 oz self-raising flour

25 g/1 oz cocoa powder

2 tbsp milk

125 g/4½ oz plain chocolate chips

Frosting

4 tbsp smooth peanut butter

5 tbsp milk

Directions

• Preheat the oven to 160°C/325°F/Gas Mark 3.

• Grease a 23 x 13 x 7.5-cm/9 x 5 x 3-inch loaf tin and line with baking paper.

• Place the butter and sugar in a large mixing bowl and using an electric hand-held whisk, beat together until pale and fluffy. Beat in the vanilla extract.

• Gradually add the eggs, beating well after each addition. Sift over the flour and cocoa powder and fold into the creamed mixture using a metal spoon. Fold in the milk and three quarters of the chocolate chips.

• Spoon the mixture into the prepared tin and gently level the surface with a small palette knife. Scatter over the rest of the chocolate chips.

• Bake in the preheated oven for 55 minutes–1 hour, or until the cake is risen, golden and firm to the touch and a skewer inserted into the centre of the cake comes out clean.

• Leave the cake in the tin for 5-10 minutes, then turn out onto a wire rack and leave to cool completely.

• For the frosting, place the peanut butter in a bowl and beat until softened. Gradually beat in the milk until smooth. Spread the frosting over the cake, allowing some to drizzle down the sides.

Chocolate & Orange Loaf Cake

Serves 8–10 per cake

Ingredients

70 g/2½ oz plain chocolate, broken into pieces

175 g/6 oz butter, softened, plus extra for
  greasing

250 g/9 oz caster sugar

5 large eggs, beaten

115 g/4 oz plain flour

2 tsp baking powder

Pinch of salt

Grated rind of 2 oranges

Directions

• Preheat the oven to 180°C/350°F/Gas Mark 4.

• Grease two 23 x 13 x 7.5-cm/9 x 5 x 3-inch loaf tins
  and line with baking paper.

• Place the chocolate in a heatproof bowl set over a
  saucepan of simmering water, taking care that the
  base of the bowl does not touch the water. Remove
  from the heat once the chocolate has melted.

• Place the butter and caster sugar in a separate bowl
  and cream with a mixer until light and fluffy. Gradually
  beat in the eggs. Sift the flour, baking powder and salt
  into the mixture and fold in.

• Transfer one third of the mixture to the melted
  chocolate and stir. Stir the orange rind into the
  remaining mixture and spread one quarter of the
  mixture evenly in each loaf tin.

• Drop spoonfuls of the chocolate mixture on top,
  dividing it between the tins, but do not smooth it
  out. Divide the remaining orange mixture between
  the tins, then, using a rounded knife, gently swirl the
  top two layers together to give a marbled effect.

• Bake in the preheated oven for 35–40 minutes or until
  a skewer or cocktail stick inserted comes out clean.
  Leave to cool in the tins for 10 minutes before
  removing.

Cinnamon Raisin Loaf Cake

Serves 8–10

Ingredients

150 g/5½ oz butter, softened, plus extra for greasing

150 g/5½ oz caster sugar

1 tsp vanilla extract

3 eggs, lightly beaten

175 g/6 oz self-raising flour

125 g/4½ oz raisins

2 tsp ground cinnamon

Directions

• Preheat the oven to 160°C/325°F/Gas Mark 3.

• Grease a 23 x 13 x 7.5-cm/9 x 5 x 3-inch loaf tin and line with baking paper.

• Place the butter and sugar in a large mixing bowl and using an electric hand-held whisk, beat together until pale and fluffy. Beat in the vanilla extract.

• Gradually add the eggs, beating well after each addition. Sift over the flour and fold into the creamed mixture using a metal spoon. Fold in the raisins.

• Transfer half the mixture to another bowl and fold in the cinnamon. Place alternate spoonfuls of the two mixtures into the prepared tin. Then swirl together with a skewer or thin bladed knife. Gently level the surface with a small palette knife.

• Bake in the preheated oven for 55 minutes – 1 hour 5 minutes, or until the cake is risen, golden and firm to the touch and a skewer inserted into the centre of the cake comes out clean.

• Leave the cake in the tin for 5–10 minutes, then turn out onto a wire rack and leave to cool completely.

Brown Sugar Walnut Loaf Cake

Serves 8–10

Ingredients

150 g/5½ oz butter, softened, plus extra for
   greasing

125 g/4½ oz light muscovado sugar

3 eggs, lightly beaten

100 g/3½ oz self-raising flour

40 g/1½ oz plain flour

85 g/3 oz walnut pieces, roughly chopped

1 small ripe banana (55 g/2 oz peeled
   weight), mashed

To serve (optional)

Walnut pieces and fresh raspberries

Directions

- Preheat the oven to 160°C/325°F/Gas Mark 3.

- Grease a 23 x 13 x 7.5-cm/9 x 5 x 3-inch loaf tin and line with baking paper.

- Place the butter and sugar in a large mixing bowl and using an electric hand-held whisk, beat together until pale and fluffy.

- Gradually add the eggs, beating well after each addition. Sift over the flours and fold into the creamed mixture using a metal spoon. Fold in the walnuts and mashed banana.

- Spoon the mixture into the prepared tin and gently level the surface with a small palette knife.

- Bake in the preheated oven for 55 minutes–1 hour, or until the cake is risen, golden and firm to the touch and a skewer inserted into the centre of the cake comes out clean.

- Leave the cake in the tin for 5-10 minutes, then turn out onto a wire rack and leave to cool completely.

- Serve the cake sliced with walnut pieces and fresh raspberries, if liked.

Marbled Loaf Cake

Serves 8–10

Ingredients

60 g/2¼ oz plain chocolate, broken into pieces

3 tbsp milk

70 g/2½ oz butter, plus extra for greasing

100 g/3½ oz caster sugar

1 egg, beaten

3 tbsp soured cream or crème fraîche

115 g/4 oz self-raising flour

½ tsp baking powder

½ tsp vanilla extract

Directions

• Preheat the oven to 160°C/325°F/Gas Mark 3.

• Grease a 23 x 13 x 7.5-cm/9 x 5 x 3-inch loaf tin and line with baking paper.

• To melt the chocolate, place it in a small heatproof bowl with the milk and set the bowl over a saucepan of simmering water. Heat gently until just melted. Remove from the heat.

• Cream together the butter and caster sugar until light and fluffy. Beat in the egg and soured cream. Sift the flour and baking powder over the mixture, then fold in using a metal spoon.

• Spoon half the mixture into a separate bowl and stir in the chocolate mixture. Add the vanilla extract to the plain mixture.

• Spoon the chocolate and vanilla mixtures alternately into the prepared loaf tin, swirling lightly with a knife for a marbled effect. Bake in the preheated oven for 40–45 minutes or until well risen and a skewer or cocktail stick inserted into the centre comes out clean.

• Leave to cool in the tin for 10 minutes, then turn out and finish cooling on a wire rack.

Ginger Loaf Cake

Serves 8–10

Ingredients

175 g/6 oz plain flour

1 tsp baking powder

1 tsp ground ginger

175 ml/6 fl oz vegetable oil , plus extra

   for greasing

115 g/4 oz soft dark brown sugar

85 g/3 oz golden syrup

3 eggs, beaten

3 pieces stem ginger in syrup, chopped,

   plus 2 tbsp syrup from jar

Sliced stem ginger, to decorate

Directions

• Preheat the oven to 180°C/350°F/Gas Mark 4.

• Grease a 23 x 13 x 7.5-cm/9 x 5 x 3-inch loaf tin and line with baking paper.

• Sift the flour, baking powder and ground ginger into a large bowl. Add in the oil, brown sugar, golden syrup and eggs and beat well to a smooth mixture. Stir in the chopped ginger.

• Pour the mixture into the prepared tin. Bake in the preheated oven for 65 minutes or until a skewer or cocktail stick inserted into centre of the cake comes out clean.

• Leave to cool in the tin for 10 minutes, then turn out on to a wire rack.

• To serve, brush the cake with the ginger syrup. Arrange the sliced ginger on top and cut into slices.

Crumb Cakes

Cinnamon Crumb Cake

Serves 9–12

Ingredients

300 g/10½ oz plain flour

1 tsp bicarbonate of soda

¾ tsp baking powder

½ tsp salt

175 g/6 oz unsalted butter, plus extra
  for greasing

300 g/10½ oz caster sugar

2 large eggs

350 g/12 oz soured cream or crème fraîche

2 tsp vanilla extract

Topping

225 g/8 oz soft light brown sugar

100 g/3½ oz caster sugar

2 tsp ground cinnamon

1 tsp ground nutmeg

½ tsp salt

225 g/8 oz unsalted butter, melted

300 g/10½ oz plain flour

Directions

• Preheat the oven to 180°C/350°F/Gas Mark 4. Grease a 33 x 23 x 5-cm/13 x 9 x 2-inch ovenproof dish.

• To make the cake mixture, sift the flour, bicarbonate of soda, baking powder and salt into a medium bowl. Using an electric mixer, beat the butter in a large bowl until smooth. Add the caster sugar and beat until light and fluffy. Add the eggs, one at a time, beating until well blended. Add the soured cream and vanilla extract and beat until blended. Add the flour mixture in 3 batches, beating until incorporated after each addition.

• Transfer the cake mixture to the prepared ovenproof dish and spread evenly with a palette knife.

• To make the topping, mix both sugars, the cinnamon, nutmeg and salt in a medium bowl. Add the melted butter and stir. Add the flour and toss with a fork until moist clumps form (the mixture will look slightly wet).

• Squeeze small handfuls of the topping mixture together to form small clumps. Drop the topping clumps evenly over the cake mixture, covering completely.

• Bake in the preheated oven for 45–50 minutes until a skewer or cocktail stick inserted into the centre comes out clean and the topping is deep golden brown and slightly crisp. Leave to cool in the dish for 30 minutes.

• Cut the cake into squares and serve slightly warm or at room temperature.

Cream Cheese Swirl Cake

Serves 9–12

Cream Cheese Mixture

225 g/8 oz cream cheese

2 tbsp icing sugar

1½ tbsp lemon juice

Cake Mixture

225 g/8 oz plain flour, plus extra for dusting

1 tsp baking powder

1 tsp bicarbonate of soda

Pinch of salt

200 g/7 oz caster sugar

115 g/4 oz butter, plus extra for
greasing

3 eggs

2 tsp vanilla extract

225 g/8 oz soured cream or crème fraîche

Topping

30 g/1 oz walnuts, finely chopped

2 tbsp caster sugar

½ tsp ground cinnamon

½ tsp ground nutmeg

Directions

• Preheat the oven to 180°C/350°F/Gas Mark 4.

• Grease and flour a 2-litre/3½-pint Bundt tin.

• To make the cream cheese mixture, beat the cream cheese, icing sugar and lemon juice in a small bowl until smooth, then set aside.

• To make the cake mixture, sift the flour, baking powder, bicarbonate of soda and salt together, then set aside.

• In a large bowl, beat the caster sugar and butter until fluffy. Add the eggs and vanilla mixing well. Add the dry ingredients alternately with the soured cream. Mix well.

• Pour half of the cake mixture into the prepared tin. Spoon the cream cheese mixture on top of the cake mixture within 1 cm/½ inch of the tin's edge. Spoon the remaining cake mixture over the filling, spreading it to the tin's edge.

• To make the topping, combine the chopped walnuts, caster sugar, ground cinnamon and nutmeg. Sprinkle it over the cake mixture.

• Bake in the preheated oven for 40–45 minutes or until a skewer or cocktail stick inserted near the centre comes out clean. Leave to cool for 10 minutes before removing from the tin. Serve warm.

Apricot Crumble Cake

Serves 9–12

Ingredients

225 g/8 oz plain flour

1 tsp baking powder

1 tsp bicarbonate of soda

¾ tsp salt

115 g/4 oz butter, plus extra for greasing

200 g/7 oz caster sugar

1 tsp vanilla extract

2 large eggs

225 ml/8 fl oz buttermilk, well-shaken

Topping

140 g/5 oz desiccated and flaked coconut

140 g/5 oz soft light brown sugar

1 tsp ground cinnamon

70 g/2½ oz butter, melted

4 tbsp apricot jam

Filling

4 tbsp apricot jam

Directions

• Preheat the oven to 180°C/350°F/Gas Mark 4.

• Line the base of a 5-cm/2-inch deep 23-cm/9-inch round cake tin with baking paper and grease the paper.

• To make the cake mixture, sift the flour, baking powder, bicarbonate of soda and salt together. Beat the butter and caster sugar together in a large bowl with an electric mixer until pale and fluffy, then beat in the vanilla extract.

• Add the eggs, one at a time, beating well after each addition, then beat in all of buttermilk with the mixer at low speed until just combined. Add flour mixture in 3 batches, mixing after each addition until just combined.

• Spoon mixture into the prepared cake tin and bake in the preheated oven for 45–50 minutes until golden and a skewer or cocktail stick inserted in the middle comes out clean.

• Leave to cool in the tin for 10 minutes, then turn out the cake on to a wire rack to cool completely. Slide cake on to a serving plate, slice the cake in half horizontally and spread with apricot jam. Sandwich the two halves back together.

• For the topping, combine the coconut, brown sugar, cinnamon, melted butter and apricot jam. Mix well. Spread on to the cake and grill for 3–5 minutes until golden brown.

Pumpkin Crumb Cake

Serves 8–10

Ingredients

225 g/8 oz plain flour

1½ tsp mixed spice

1 tsp bicarbonate of soda

1 tsp baking powder

¾ tsp salt

115 g/4 oz unsalted butter, plus extra for greasing

250 g/9 oz caster sugar

3 large eggs

225 g/8 oz canned pumpkin purée or
puréed butternut squash

1 tsp vanilla extract

5 tbsp milk

85 g/3 oz chopped walnuts (optional)

Topping

60 g/2¼ oz rolled oats, plus 2 tbsp

60 g/2¼ oz plain flour

115 g/4 oz soft light brown sugar

½ tsp cinnamon

85 g/3 oz unsalted butter

Directions

• Preheat the oven to 180°C/350°F/Gas Mark 4.

• Grease a 23 x 13 x 7.5-cm/9 x 5 x 3-inch loaf tin and line with baking paper.

• To make the topping, combine the 60 g/2¼ oz oats, the flour, the brown sugar and cinnamon in a processor. Add the butter and cut in until crumbly. Transfer the mixture to a medium bowl. Stir in the remaining 2 tablespoons of oats. Set to one side.

• Sift the flour, mixed spice, bicarbonate of soda, baking powder and salt into a bowl.

• In a separate bowl, beat the butter with an electric mixer until smooth. Gradually beat in the caster sugar and the eggs, one at a time. Add the pumpkin purée and vanilla extract.

• Gradually beat the dry ingredients into the wet mixture. Slowly add the milk and stir in the walnuts (optional). Transfer the mixture to the prepared tin and spread with the topping.

• Bake in the preheated oven for about 55 minutes until a skewer or cocktail stick inserted into centre comes out clean. Leave to cool in the tin for 15 minutes.

• Turn the cake out on to a rack and cool completely.

Blueberry Crumb Cake

Serves 9–12

Ingredients

225 g/8 oz plain flour

200 g/7 oz caster sugar

2 tsp baking powder

¾ tsp bicarbonate of soda

1 tsp salt

1½ tsp cinnamon

1 tsp nutmeg

175 g/6 oz unsalted butter, plus extra
   for greasing

2 large eggs, lightly beaten

225 g/8 oz soured cream or crème fraîche

4 tbsp milk

2 tsp vanilla extract

450 g/1 lb fresh blueberries

2 tsp lemon extract

Topping

25 g/1 oz unsalted butter

125 g/4½ oz plain flour

2 tbsp caster sugar

Directions

• Preheat the oven to 190°C/375°F/Gas Mark 5.

• Grease a 33 x 23 x 5-cm/13 x 9 x 2-inch baking tin and line with baking paper.

• Sift the flour, caster sugar, baking powder, bicarbonate of soda, salt, cinnamon and nutmeg together and set aside.

• Rub the butter into the flour with your fingertips until the mixture resembles fine breadcrumbs.

• Whisk the eggs, soured cream, milk and vanilla together and add to the flour mixture, stirring until combined.

• Fold the blueberries and lemon extract into the mixture before adding the mixture to the prepared baking tin.

• To make the crumble topping, rub the butter into the flour until the mixture resembles fine breadcrumbs. Add the caster sugar. Sprinkle over the cake mixture.

• Bake in the preheated oven for 40–50 minutes until the cake is golden and a skewer or cocktail stick inserted into the centre comes out clean. Leave the cake to cool in the tin for 20 minutes before serving.

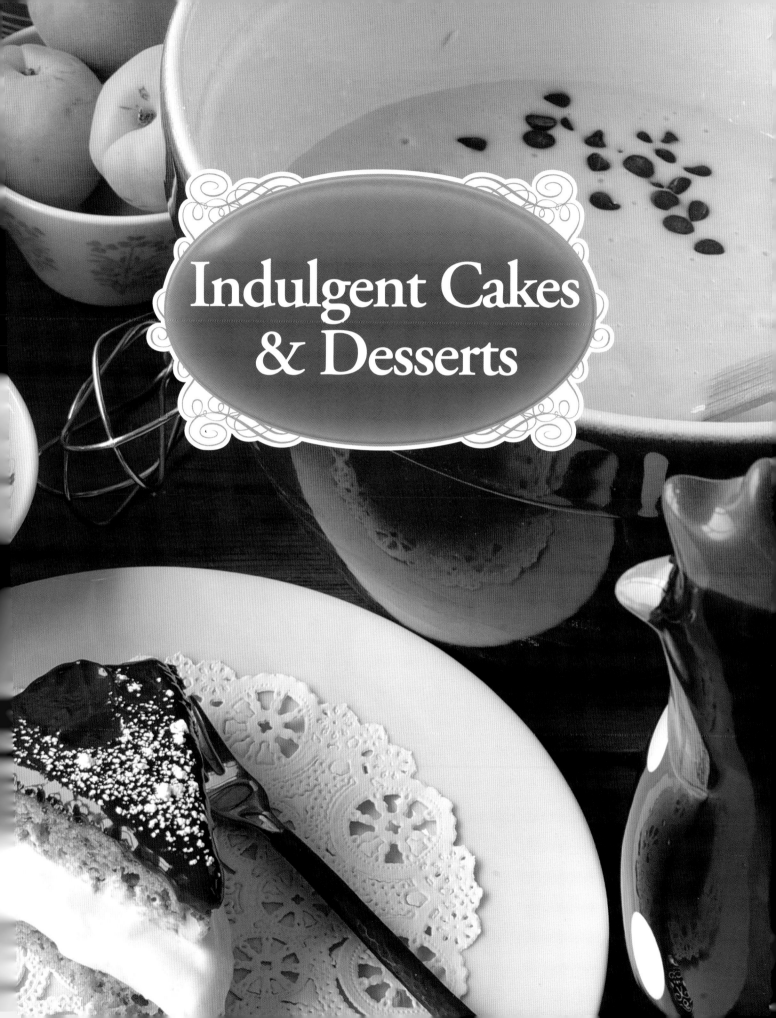

Indulgent Cakes & Desserts

Mocha Layer Cake

Serves 8–10

Ingredients

225 g/8 oz self-raising flour

¼ tsp baking powder

25 g/1 oz cocoa powder

100 g/3½ oz caster sugar

2 eggs, beaten

2 tbsp golden syrup

150 ml/5 fl oz vegetable oil, plus extra
  for greasing

150 ml/5 fl oz milk

Filling and Topping

1 tsp instant coffee powder

1 tbsp boiling water

300 ml/10 fl oz double cream

2 tbsp icing sugar

Decoration

35 g/1¼ oz chocolate, grated and curled

Icing sugar, for dusting

Directions

• Preheat the oven to 180°C/350°F/Gas Mark 4.

• Grease 3 x 20-cm/8-inch round cake tins and line with baking paper.

• To make the cake mixture, sift the flour, baking powder and cocoa powder into a large mixing bowl. Stir in the caster sugar. Make a well in the centre and stir in the eggs, golden syrup, oil and milk. Beat with a wooden spoon, gradually mixing in the dry ingredients to make a smooth mixture.

• Divide the cake mixture between the prepared tins. Bake in the preheated oven for 35–45 minutes or until springy to the touch.

• Leave to cool in the tins for 5 minutes, then turn out on to a wire rack to finish cooling.

• For the filling and topping, dissolve the instant coffee in the boiling water and place in a bowl with the cream and icing sugar. Whip until the cream just holds its shape.

• Use half of the cream to sandwich the 3 cakes together. Spread the remaining cream over the top and sides of the cake.

• To decorate, lightly press the grated chocolate into the cream around the edge of the cake. Transfer to a serving plate. Arrange the chocolate curls over the top of the cake and dust lightly with icing sugar.

Chocolate Chiffon Tart

Serves 8–10

Filling

225 ml/8 fl oz milk

2 tsp powdered gelatine

100 g/3½ oz caster sugar

2 eggs, separated

140 g/5oz plain chocolate, broken into pieces

1 tsp vanilla extract

150 ml/5 fl oz double cream

Nut Base

275 g/9¾ oz Brazil nuts

55 g/2 oz caster sugar

55 g/2 oz butter, melted, plus extra
   for greasing

Decoration

2 tbsp chopped Brazil nuts

Directions

- Preheat the oven to 200°C/400°F/Gas Mark 6 and grease a 23-cm/9-inch tart tin.

- To make the nut base, place the Brazil nuts in a food processor and process until ground. Add the sugar and melted butter and process to combine.

- Tip the mixture into the prepared tin and press it on to the base and side with a spoon. Bake in the preheated oven for 8–10 minutes or until light golden brown. Set aside to cool.

- For the filling, pour the milk into a heatproof bowl and sprinkle the gelatine over the surface. Leave to soften for 2 minutes, then set over a saucepan of gently simmering water. Stir in half of the caster sugar, the egg

yolks and chocolate. Stir constantly over a low heat for 4–5 minutes until the gelatine has dissolved and the chocolate has melted. Remove from the heat and beat until the mixture is smooth. Stir in the vanilla extract and chill in the refrigerator for 45–60 minutes.

- Whip the cream until stiff peaks form. Fold all but 3 tablespoons into the chocolate mixture.

- Whisk the egg whites in a separate bowl until soft peaks form. Add 2 tablespoons of the caster sugar and whisk until stiff peaks form. Fold in the remaining caster sugar, then fold the egg whites into the chocolate mixture. Pour the filling into the nut base and chill in the fridge for 3 hours. Decorate the pie with the remaining whipped cream and the chopped nuts before serving.

Chocolate Fudge Cake

Serves 8–10

Ingredients

175 g/6 oz butter, softened, plus extra
  for greasing

200 g/7 oz caster sugar

3 eggs, beaten

3 tbsp golden syrup

3 tbsp ground almonds

115 g/4 oz self-raising flour

Pinch of salt

25 g/1 oz cocoa powder

Icing

140 g/5 oz plain chocolate, broken into pieces

55 g/2 oz soft light brown sugar

225 g/8 oz butter, diced

5 tbsp evaporated milk

½ tsp vanilla extract

Directions

- Preheat the oven to 180°C/350°F/Gas Mark 4.

- Grease and line 2 x 20-cm/8-inch round cake tins with baking paper.

- To make the cakes, put the butter and caster sugar in a bowl and beat together until light and fluffy. Gradually beat in the eggs. Stir in the golden syrup and ground almonds. Sift the flour, salt and cocoa into a separate bowl, then fold into the cake mixture. Add a little water, if necessary, to make a dropping consistency.

- Spoon the cake mixture into the prepared tins and bake in the preheated oven for 30–35 minutes or until springy to the touch and a skewer or cocktail stick inserted in the centre comes out clean.

- Leave to cool in the tins for 5 minutes, then turn out on to wire racks to cool completely.

- To make the icing, place the chocolate, brown sugar, butter, evaporated milk and vanilla extract in a heavy-based saucepan. Heat gently, stirring constantly, until melted. Pour into a bowl and leave to cool. Cover and leave to chill in the refrigerator for 1 hour.

- When the cakes have cooled, sandwich them together with half the icing. Spread the remaining icing over the top and sides of the cake, swirling it to give a wavy appearance.

Coffee & Walnut Swirl

Serves 6–8

Ingredients

butter for greasing

3 eggs

1 egg white

100 g/3½ oz caster sugar, plus extra
   for dusting

1 tsp coffee extract

60 g/2¼ oz plain flour, sifted

30 g/1 oz walnuts, finely chopped, plus extra
   roughly chopped for decoration

Filling

175 ml/6 fl oz double cream

50 g/1¾ oz icing sugar, plus extra for dusting

1 tbsp coffee liqueur

Directions

- Preheat the oven to 200°C/400°F/Gas Mark 6.

- Grease a 33 x 23-cm/13 x 9-inch Swiss roll tin and line with baking paper.

- To make the sponge cake, place the eggs, egg white and caster sugar in a bowl over a saucepan of very hot water. Whisk with an electric mixer until pale and thick enough to leave a trail. Whisk in the coffee extract, then fold in the flour and the finely chopped walnuts lightly with a metal spoon.

- Spoon the mixture into the prepared tin, spreading evenly. Bake in the preheated oven for 12–15 minutes until golden brown and firm.

- Sprinkle a sheet of baking paper with caster sugar. Turn out the sponge on to the paper and peel off the baking paper. Trim the edges.

- Quickly roll up the sponge from one short side, with the paper inside. Leave to cool completely.

- For the filling, place the cream, icing sugar and liqueur in a bowl and whisk until the mixture begins to hold its shape.

- Carefully unroll the sponge, remove the paper and spread the cream filling over. Roll up carefully.

- Serve dusted with icing sugar and topped with roughly chopped walnuts.

Banana Crunch Cake

Serves 8–10

Ingredients

225 g/8 oz can crushed pineapple in juice

275 g/9¾ oz plain flour

250 g/9 oz caster sugar

1 tsp ground cinnamon

1 tsp bicarbonate of soda

3 eggs, beaten

225 ml/8 fl oz vegetable oil, plus extra

   for greasing

115 g/4 oz pecan nuts, roughly chopped

225 g/8 oz ripe bananas (peeled weight), mashed

Icing

175 g/6 oz cream cheese

115 g/4 oz unsalted butter

1 tsp vanilla extract

450 g/1 lb icing sugar

Chopped pecan nuts, to decorate

Directions

• Preheat the oven to 180°C/350°F/Gas Mark 4.

• Lightly grease 3 x 23-cm/9-inch round cake tins and line with baking paper.

• Drain the pineapple, reserving 4 tablespoons of the juice. Set aside.

• To make the cake, sift together the flour, sugar, cinnamon and bicarbonate of soda into a large bowl. Add the eggs, oil, pecan nuts, bananas, pineapple and pineapple juice and stir with a wooden spoon until evenly mixed.

• Divide the mixture between the prepared tins, spreading it evenly. Bake in the preheated oven for 25–30 minutes or until golden brown and firm to the touch.

• Remove the cakes from the oven and leave to cool for 10 minutes in the tins before turning out on to wire racks to cool.

• For the icing, beat together the cream cheese, butter and vanilla extract in a bowl until smooth. Sift in the icing sugar and mix until smooth.

• Sandwich the cakes together with half of the icing, spread the remaining icing over the top, then sprinkle with chopped pecan nuts to decorate.

Carrot Cake

Serves 8–10

Ingredients

175 g/6 oz plain flour

1 tsp baking powder

1 tsp ground cinnamon

½ tsp ground ginger

175 g/6 oz unsalted butter, plus extra
   for greasing

175 g/6 oz soft light brown sugar

3 eggs, beaten

2 tbsp orange juice

175 g/6 oz carrots, roughly grated

55 g/2 oz pecan nuts, chopped

Icing

55 g/2 oz cream cheese

275 g/9¾ oz icing sugar

Finely grated rind of 1 orange

1 tbsp orange juice, plus extra if necessary

Pecan halves, to decorate

Directions

• Preheat the oven to 160°C/325°F/Gas Mark 3.

• Grease and line a 23-cm/9-inch Swiss roll tin with
  baking paper.

• To make the cake, sift the flour, baking powder,
  cinnamon and ginger into a bowl and add the butter,
  brown sugar and eggs. Beat well until smooth, then stir
  in the orange juice, carrots and chopped pecan nuts.

• Spoon the mixture into the prepared tin and
  spread the top level. Bake in the preheated oven for
  1 hour–1 hour 10 minutes or until well risen, firm
  and golden brown.

• Leave to cool in the tin for 10 minutes, then turn
  out on to a wire rack to finish cooling.

• For the icing, put all the ingredients, except the
  pecan halves, into a bowl and beat until smooth
  and thick, adding more orange juice if necessary.
  Spread over the top of the cake and decorate with
  the pecan halves.

Rich Chocolate Layer Cake

Serves 8–10

Ingredients

85 g/3 oz plain chocolate, broken into pieces

2 tbsp milk

175 g/6 oz plain flour

1 tsp baking powder

175 g/6 oz unsalted butter, plus extra
   for greasing

175 g/6 oz soft light brown sugar

3 eggs, beaten

1 tsp vanilla extract

Icing

250 g/9 oz plain chocolate, broken into pieces

225 ml/8 fl oz double cream

2 tbsp dark rum

Grated chocolate, to decorate

Directions

• Preheat the oven to 180°C/350°F/Gas Mark 4.

• Grease and line 3 x 20-cm/8-inch round cake tins with baking paper.

• Put the chocolate and milk into a small saucepan and heat gently, without boiling, until melted. Stir and remove from the heat.

• Sift the flour and baking powder into a large bowl and add the butter, brown sugar, eggs and vanilla extract. Beat until smooth, then stir in the chocolate mixture.

• Divide the mixture between the prepared tins and smooth the tops level. Bake in the preheated oven for 20–25 minutes or until risen and firm to the touch.

• Leave to cool in the tins for 5 minutes, then turn out and finish cooling on wire racks.

• For the icing, melt the chocolate with the cream and rum in a small saucepan over a low heat. Remove from the heat and leave to cool, stirring occasionally, until it reaches a spreadable consistency.

• Sandwich the cakes together with about a third of the icing, then spread the remainder over the top and sides of the cake, swirling with a palette knife. Sprinkle with grated chocolate and leave to set.

Indulgent Cakes & Desserts   **173**

Strawberry Layer Cake

Serves 6–8

Ingredients

175 g/6 oz plain flour

1½ tsp baking powder

175 g/6 oz unsalted butter, plus extra

   for greasing

175 g/6 oz caster sugar

3 eggs, beaten

1 tsp vanilla extract

2 tbsp milk

Filling

300 g/10½ oz fresh strawberries

225 g/8 oz mascarpone cheese

Icing sugar, for dusting

Directions

• Preheat the oven to 180°C/350°F/Gas Mark 4.

• Grease a 33 x 23-cm/13 x 9-inch Swiss roll tin and line with baking paper.

• To make the cake, sift the flour and baking powder into a large bowl and add the butter, caster sugar, eggs and vanilla extract. Beat well until the mixture is smooth, then beat in the milk.

• Spoon the mixture into the prepared tin and smooth into the corners with a palette knife. Bake in the preheated oven for 15–20 minutes or until risen, firm and golden brown. Leave to cool in the tin.

• When the cake is cold, cut crossways into three rectangles. Hull and chop the strawberries, reserving 4 for decoration. Stir the chopped strawberries into the mascarpone and use to sandwich the cakes together.

• To serve, dust the cake with icing sugar. Hull and slice the reserved strawberries and arrange on top.

Double Chocolate Mint Cake

Serves 8–10

Ingredients

150 g/5½ oz plain flour

2 tbsp cocoa powder

1 tsp baking powder

175 g/6 oz unsalted butter, plus extra
for greasing

200 g/7 oz caster sugar

3 eggs, beaten

1 tbsp milk

12 chocolate mint sticks, chopped

Filling and Decoration

115 g/4 oz chocolate spread

Chocolate mint sticks, to decorate

Directions

• Preheat the oven to 180°C/350°F/Gas Mark 4.

• Grease 2 x 20-cm/8-inch cake tins and line with baking paper.

• To make the cake, sift the flour, cocoa powder and baking powder into a bowl and beat in the butter, caster sugar and eggs, mixing until smooth. Stir in the milk and chocolate mint pieces.

• Spread the mixture into the tins. Bake in the preheated oven for 25–30 minutes until risen and firm. Leave to cool in the tins for 2 minutes, then turn out on to a wire rack to finish cooling.

• Sandwich the cakes together with the chocolate spread, then drizzle some of the chocolate spread over the top.

• Decorate the cake with chocolate mint sticks and drizzle a little more chocolate spread on top.

White Chocolate Mocha Cake

Serves 8–10

Ingredients

40 g/1½ oz unsalted butter, plus extra
   for greasing

85 g/3 oz white chocolate, broken into pieces

125 g/4½ oz caster sugar

4 large eggs, beaten

2 tbsp very strong black coffee

1 tsp vanilla extract

115 g/4 oz plain flour

Icing

175 g/6 oz white chocolate, broken into pieces

85 g/3 oz unsalted butter

115 g/4 oz soured cream or crème fraîche

115 g/4 oz icing sugar, sifted

1 tbsp coffee liqueur or very strong
   black coffee

White chocolate curls, to decorate

Directions

• Preheat the oven to 180°C/350°F/Gas Mark 4.

• Grease 2 x 20-cm/8-inch round cake tins and line with baking paper.

• Put the butter and chocolate in a heatproof bowl set over a saucepan of hot, but not simmering, water and leave on very low heat until just melted.

• To make the cakes, place the sugar, eggs, coffee and vanilla extract in a large bowl set over a saucepan of hot water and whisk with an electric mixer until the mixture is pale and thick. Remove from the heat and sift in the flour. Fold in the butter and chocolate mixture and divide between the prepared tins.

• Bake in the preheated for 25–30 minutes until risen, golden brown and springy to the touch. Leave to cool in the tins for 2 minutes before turning out on to a wire rack to cool.

• For the icing, place the chocolate and butter in a heatproof bowl set over a saucepan of hot water and heat gently until melted. Remove from the heat, stir in the soured cream, then add the icing sugar and coffee liqueur and mix until smooth. Chill the icing for at least 30 minutes, stirring occasionally, until thick and glossy.

• Use about one third of the icing to sandwich the cakes together. Spread the remainder over the top and sides, swirling with a palette knife. Arrange the chocolate curls over the top of the cake and leave to set.

Pumpkin Sandwich Cake

Serves 8–10

Ingredients

butter for greasing

100 g/3½ oz plain flour

1½ tsp mixed spice

1 tsp baking powder

¼ tsp salt

3 eggs

200 g/7 oz caster sugar

4 tbsp canned pumpkin purée or

   puréed butternut squash

Filling

125 ml/4 fl oz whipping cream

115 g/4 oz cream cheese

60 g/2¼ oz icing sugar, plus extra for dusting

Icing

125 ml/4 fl oz whipping cream

175 g/6 oz plain chocolate (at least

   70% cocoa solids), broken into pieces

Directions

• Preheat the oven to 190°C/375°F/Gas Mark 5. Grease 2 x 20-cm/8-inch round cake tins and line with baking paper.

• To make the cakes, in a large bowl combine the flour, mixed spice, baking powder and salt, then set aside.

• In a second bowl, beat the eggs and caster sugar with an electric mixer on medium-high speed until thick. Beat in the pumpkin. Add to the flour and mix until combined.

• Spread the cake mixture in the prepared tins. Bake in the preheated oven for 16–18 minutes or until a skewer or cocktail stick inserted into the centre comes out clean. Leave to cool in the tins for 10 minutes, then remove and cool on a wire rack thoroughly.

• For the filling, in a chilled mixing bowl beat the cream to soft peaks, then set aside. In a separate bowl, beat the cream cheese until smooth and mix in the icing sugar. Fold in the whipped cream.

• To assemble, place one cake layer on a serving platter. Spread the cream cheese mixture evenly over the base cake layer. Top with the second cake layer.

• For the icing, pour the whipping cream into a small saucepan and bring just to boiling over a medium heat. Remove from the heat and pour over the chocolate, pieces. Leave to stand for 5 minutes. Stir until smooth. Leave to cool for 15 minutes, then pour over the top and sides of the cake. Dust lightly with extra icing sugar.

Angel Food Cake

Serves 8–10

Ingredients

oil for greasing

8 large egg whites

1 tsp cream of tartar

1 tsp almond extract

150 g/5½ oz caster sugar

115 g/4 oz plain flour, plus extra for dusting

Topping

250 g/9 oz mixed berries, such as raspberries, strawberries and redcurrants

1 tbsp lemon juice

2 tbsp icing sugar

Directions

- Preheat the oven to 160°C/325°F/Gas Mark 3.

- Brush the inside of a 2-litre/3½-pint Bundt tin with oil and dust lightly with flour.

- To make the cake, in a large grease-free bowl, whisk the egg whites until they hold soft peaks. Add the cream of tartar and whisk again until the whites are stiff but not dry.

- Whisk in the almond extract, then add the caster sugar a tablespoon at a time, whisking hard between each addition. Sift in the flour and fold in lightly and evenly.

- Spoon the mixture into the prepared cake tin and tap on the work surface to remove any large air bubbles. Bake in the preheated oven for 40–45 minutes or until golden brown and firm to the touch.

- Run the tip of a small knife around the edge of the cake to loosen from the tin. Leave to cool in the tin for 10 minutes, then turn out on to a wire rack to finish cooling.

- Place the berries, lemon juice and icing sugar in a saucepan and heat gently until the sugar has dissolved. Serve on top of the cake.

New York Cheesecake

Serves 8–10

Base

115 g/4 oz butter, plus extra for greasing

200 g/7 oz finely crushed digestive biscuits

1 tbsp caster sugar

Filling

900 g/2 lb cream cheese

250 g/9 oz caster sugar

2 tbsp plain flour

1 tsp vanilla extract

Finely grated rind of 1 orange

Finely grated rind of 1 lemon

3 eggs

2 egg yolks

300 ml/10 fl oz double cream

Directions

• Preheat the oven to 180°C/350°F/Gas Mark 4.

• Grease a 23-cm/9-inch round, springform cake tin and line with baking paper.

• To make the base, place a small saucepan over a low heat, melt the butter and remove from heat. Stir in the crushed biscuits and caster sugar. Press the biscuit mixture into the base of the cake tin.

• Place in the preheated oven and bake for 10 minutes. Remove and leave to cool in the tin.

• Increase the oven temperature to 200°C/400°F/Gas Mark 6. With an electric mixer beat the cream cheese until creamy and gradually add the caster sugar and flour and beat until smooth.

• Beat in the vanilla extract, orange and lemon rind, then beat in the eggs and egg yolks one at a time. Finally beat in the cream. The mixture should be light and airy.

• Grease the sides of the cake tin and pour in the filling. Transfer to the preheated oven and bake for 15 minutes. Reduce the heat to 110°C/225°F/Gas Mark ¼ and bake for an additional 30 minutes. Turn the oven off and leave in the oven to cool for 2 hours.

• Cover with clingfilm and refrigerate overnight.

Brownie Cheesecake

Serves 8–10

Base

115 g/4 oz unsalted butter, plus extra

   for greasing

175 g/6 oz plain chocolate, broken into pieces

200 g/7 oz caster sugar

2 eggs, beaten

4 tbsp milk

115 g/4 oz plain flour, plus extra for dusting

Topping

450 g/1 lb cream cheese

125 g/4½ oz caster sugar

3 eggs, beaten

1 tsp vanilla extract

115 g/4 oz natural yogurt

Decoration

Melted chocolate, for drizzling

Chocolate-dipped strawberries, to serve

Directions

• Preheat the oven to 180°C/350°F/Gas Mark 4.

• Lightly grease and flour a 23-cm/9-inch round springform cake tin.

• To make the base, melt the butter and chocolate in a saucepan over a low heat, stirring frequently, until smooth. Remove from the heat and beat in the caster sugar.

• Add the eggs and milk, beating well. Stir in the flour, mixing just until blended. Spoon into the prepared tin, spreading evenly.

• Bake in the preheated oven for 25 minutes. Remove from the oven and reduce the oven temperature to 160°C/325°F/Gas Mark 3.

• For the topping, beat the cream cheese, sugar, eggs and vanilla extract together until well blended. Stir in the yogurt, then pour into the tin. Bake for an additional 45–55 minutes or until the centre is almost set.

• Run a knife around the edge of the cheesecake to loosen from the tin. Leave to cool before removing from the tin. Chill in the refrigerator for 4 hours or overnight before cutting into slices.

• Drizzle with melted chocolate and serve with chocolate-dipped strawberries.

Rose Blossom Cake

Serves 8–10

Ingredients

175 g/6 oz unsalted butter, plus extra
  for greasing

300 g/10½ oz caster sugar

3 large eggs

225 g/8 oz plain flour

1 tsp baking powder

1 tsp bicarbonate of soda

1 tsp salt

225 g/8 oz plain yogurt

2 tsp vanilla extract

1 tsp almond extract

Buttercream Icing and Filling

225 g/8 oz unsalted butter, softened

600 g/1 lb 5 oz icing sugar

2–3 tbsp milk

1 tsp vanilla extract

Decoration

550 g/1 lb 4 oz ready-to-roll
  fondant icing

Red food colouring

Crystallized rose petals

Directions

• Preheat the oven to 180°C/350°F/Gas Mark 4. Grease a 15-cm/6-inch round cake tin and a 20-cm/8-inch round cake tin and line with baking paper.

• Cream the butter and caster sugar until fluffy. Beat in the eggs, one at a time. Slowly sift in the flour, baking powder, bicarbonate of soda and salt and fold in.

• Mix the yogurt, vanilla and almond extract together in a separate bowl. Add slowly to the mixture, mixing until well blended. Pour into the prepared tins.

• Bake in the preheated oven for 35 minutes or until a skewer or cocktail stick inserted into the centre comes out clean. Leave to cool.

• To make the buttercream, beat the butter until fluffy and add the icing sugar, milk and vanilla, beating until pale and creamy. If the mixture seems too thick add more milk.

• Slice both cakes in half horizontally then sandwich together with a layer of buttercream. Lightly ice the sides and top of each cake separately with the remaining buttercream.

• Dye the fondant pink by kneading in a very small drop of food colouring. Roll out into two rounds and smooth the icing over each cake. Trim. Place the smaller cake on top of the larger one.

• Decorate the cake with the crystallized rose petals or cut some of the fondant trimmings into petal shapes.

Lace Cake

Serves 8–10

Ingredients

225 g/8 oz unsalted butter, plus extra
   for greasing
600 g/1 lb 5 oz caster sugar
4 large eggs
125 g/4½ oz cocoa powder
500 g/1 lb 2 oz plain flour
2 tsp baking powder
2 tsp bicarbonate of soda
1 tsp salt
450 ml/16 fl oz milk
2 tsp vanilla extract
225 ml/8 fl oz boiling water

Dark Chocolate Icing

225 g/8 oz unsalted butter, softened
60 g/2¼ oz cocoa powder
350 g/12 oz icing sugar
125 ml/4 fl oz milk
1 tsp vanilla extract

Decoration

25 g/1 oz cocoa powder, for dusting
1 20-cm/8-inch round doily or plastic stencil
25 g/1 oz icing sugar, for dusting
Chocolate-covered coffee beans
Silver dragées

Directions

• Preheat the oven to 180°C/350°F/Gas Mark 4. Lightly grease a 23-cm/9-inch round cake tin and line with baking paper.

• Cream the butter and sugar together until smooth and light in colour. Beat in one egg at a time, mixing well.

• Sift the cocoa, flour, baking powder, bicarbonate of soda and salt together into a separate bowl. Slowly add to the butter and sugar mixture, mixing well. Mix in the milk, vanilla extract and water. Pour the mixture evenly into the prepared tin.

• Bake in the preheated oven for 30 minutes or until a skewer or cocktail stick inserted into the centre comes out clean. Remove and leave to cool.

• To make the icing, beat the butter until fluffy. Sift the cocoa and icing sugar together and add to the butter, together with the milk and vanilla extract. Beat until creamy and spreadable.

• Slice the cake in half horizontally and sandwich together with the icing.

• Just before serving, fill a small fine-mesh sieve with cocoa. Dust the cake by gently tapping as you move the sieve over the cake. Then place the doily or stencil on the cake, fill the clean sieve with icing sugar and dust the cake. Carefully remove the doily – the lace pattern will show up on the cake.

• Decorate with coffee beans and silver dragées.

Pies

Lemon Meringue Pie

Serves 8

Pastry

500 g/1lb 2 oz ready-made shortcrust
   pastry
flour for dusting

Filling

3 tbsp cornflour
100 g/3½ oz caster sugar
Finely grated rind of 3 lemons

300 ml/10 fl oz cold water
150 ml/5 fl oz lemon juice
3 egg yolks
55 g/2 oz butter, diced, plus
   extra for greasing

Meringue

3 egg whites
200 g/7 oz caster sugar

Directions

• Preheat oven to 200°C/400°F/Gas Mark 6. Grease a 25-cm/10-inch fluted tart tin.

• Roll out the pastry on a lightly floured surface into a round 5 cm/2 inches larger than the tart tin. Ease the pastry into the tart tin and press down lightly into the corners and trim the edge. Prick the base with a fork and chill in the refrigerator for 20–30 minutes.

• Line the pastry case with baking paper and fill with baking weights or dried beans. Bake on a preheated baking tray for 15 minutes. Remove the weights and paper and return to the oven for 10 minutes or until the pastry is dry and just coloured. Remove from the oven and reduce the temperature to 150°C/300°F/ Gas Mark 2.

• To make the filling, put the cornflour, caster sugar and lemon rind in a saucepan. Gradually add the water and the lemon juice. Bring the mixture to the boil, stirring constantly. Simmer until smooth and glossy.

• Remove from the heat and beat in the egg yolks, one at a time, then beat in the butter. Leave to cool before spooning into the pastry case.

• For the meringue, whisk the egg whites with an electric mixer until soft peaks form. Add the caster sugar gradually, whisking well with each addition. Spoon over the filling. Swirl the meringue into peaks. Bake in the preheated oven for 20–30 minutes or until the meringue is crispy and pale gold but still soft in the centre. Cool before serving.

Sweet Potato Pie

Serves 8

Pastry

150 g/5½ oz plain flour

½ tsp salt

¼ tsp caster sugar

25 g/1 oz butter, diced, plus extra for greasing

40 g/1½ oz vegetable fat

2–2½ tbsp ice-cold water

Filling

650 g/1 lb 7 oz cooked sweet potatoes, mashed

3 large eggs, beaten

115 g/4 oz soft dark brown sugar

350 ml/12 fl oz evaporated milk

40 g/1½ oz butter, melted

2 tsp vanilla extract

1 tsp ground cinnamon,

    plus extra for dusting

1 tsp ground nutmeg

½ tsp salt

Freshly whipped cream, to serve

Directions

• Preheat oven to 220°C/425°F/Gas Mark 7. Grease a 23-cm/9-inch tart tin.

• To make the pastry, sift the flour, salt and caster sugar into a bowl. Add the butter and vegetable fat to the bowl and rub in with the fingertips until fine crumbs form. Sprinkle over 2 tablespoons of the water and mix with a fork until a soft dough forms, adding the extra water, if necessary. Wrap in clingfilm and chill for at least 1 hour.

• To make the filling, put the sweet potatoes into a separate bowl and beat in the eggs and sugar until very smooth. Beat in the remaining ingredients, except the whipped cream, then set aside.

• Roll out the pastry on a lightly floured surface into a thin 28-cm/11-inch round and line the tart tin. Trim off the excess pastry and press the floured tines of a fork around the edge.

• Prick the base of the pastry case all over with the fork and place crumpled kitchen foil in the centre. Bake for 12 minutes or until golden.

• Remove the pastry case from the oven, take out the foil, pour the filling into the case and return to the oven for an additional 10 minutes. Reduce the oven temperature to 160°C/325°F/Gas Mark 3 and bake for a further 35 minutes or until a knife inserted into the centre comes out clean. Leave to cool on a wire rack. Serve warm with whipped cream and sprinkled with cinnamon.

Spiced Pumpkin Pie

Serves 8

Pastry

115 g/4 oz plain flour, plus extra for dusting

¼ tsp baking powder

Pinch each ground cinnamon, nutmeg and cloves

1 tsp salt

100 g/3½ oz caster sugar

55 g/2 oz unsalted butter, plus extra
for greasing

1 egg

Filling

425 g/15 oz canned pumpkin purée or puréed
butternut squash

550 g/1 lb 4 oz sweetened condensed milk

2 eggs

1 tsp mixed spice

½ tsp vanilla extract

1 tbsp soft light brown sugar

Topping

2 tbsp plain flour

55 g/2 oz soft light brown sugar

1 tsp mixed spice

25 g/1 oz unsalted butter

70 g/2½ oz pecan nuts, chopped

70 g/2½ oz walnuts, chopped

Directions

• Preheat the oven to 220°C/425°F/Gas Mark 7. Grease a 23-cm/9-inch round tart tin.

• To make the pastry, sift the flour and baking powder into a large bowl. Stir in the cinnamon, nutmeg, cloves, salt and caster sugar.

• Rub in the butter with your fingertips until the mixture resembles fine breadcrumbs, then make a well in the centre. Lightly beat the egg and pour it into the well. Mix together with a wooden spoon, then use your hands to shape the pastry into a ball.

• Place the pastry on a lightly floured surface and roll out to a round large enough to line the tart tin. Use it to

line the tin, then trim the edges. Cover with clingfilm and chill in the refrigerator for 30 minutes.

• To make the filling, put the pumpkin purée in a large bowl. Stir in the condensed milk and the eggs. Add the mixed spice, then stir in the vanilla extract and brown sugar. Pour into the pastry case and bake in the preheated oven for 15 minutes.

• To make the topping, combine the flour, brown sugar and mixed spice in a bowl. Rub in the butter, then stir in the nuts.

• Remove the pie from the oven and reduce the heat to 180°C/350°F/Gas Mark 4. Sprinkle the topping over the pie and bake for an additional 35 minutes. Serve warm.

Simple Apple Pie

Serves 8

Pastry

butter for greasing

2 sheets ready-made shortcrust pastry,
   thawed if frozen

flour for dusting

1 beaten egg, for glazing

Filling

6 cooking apples

5 tbsp lemon juice

200 g/7 oz caster sugar

3 tbsp cornflour

Pinch of nutmeg

½ tsp cinnamon

25 g/1 oz butter

Directions

• Preheat oven to 190°C/375°F/Gas Mark 5.

• Grease a 23-cm/9-inch pie dish.

• Roll one sheet of pastry on a lightly floured surface to form the base of the pie. It should be rolled large enough to cover the dish with 5 cm/2 inches to spare all around. Place and press into the dish.

• For the filling, peel, core and slice the apples into thin slices. Toss the apple slices with the lemon juice in a large mixing bowl. Add the rest of the filling ingredients, except the butter, and mix until well combined.

• Spoon the apple mixture into the base pastry case. Dot the top of the apples with the butter.

• Roll out the second piece of pastry and cover the apple filling.

• Press the two pieces of dough together with your fingers. Pinch the edges so that both edges are sealed all the way around the dish.

• Cut a few slashes in the pastry top so the steam can escape, then brush the pastry top with the beaten egg. Bake in the preheated oven for 40-45 minutes until the pastry is nicely browned and the apples are tender when tested with a small knife through the slits on the top. If the pastry begins to brown too quickly, cover with foil.

• Serve warm or cooled.

Cherry Pie

Serves 8

Pastry

115 g/4 oz plain flour, plus extra for dusting

¼ tsp baking powder

½ tsp mixed spice

½ tsp salt

55 g/2 oz caster sugar

55 g/2 oz unsalted butter, plus

extra for greasing

1 egg, beaten, plus extra for glazing

Filling

900 g/2 lb stoned fresh cherries or drained

canned cherries

100 g/3½ oz caster sugar

½ tsp almond extract

2 tsp cherry brandy

¼ tsp mixed spice

2 tbsp cornflour

2 tbsp water

25 g/1 oz unsalted butter

Directions

• Preheat the oven to 220°C/425°F/Gas Mark 7. Grease a 23-cm/9-inch round pie dish.

• To make the pastry, sift the flour and baking powder into a large bowl. Stir in the mixed spice, salt and caster sugar. Rub in the butter with your fingertips until the mixture resembles fine breadcrumbs. Add the beaten egg and mix to a firm mixture. Cut the mixture in half and roll each half into a ball. Roll out one half of the pastry and line the dish.

• To make the filling, put half of the cherries and the caster sugar in a large saucepan. Bring to a simmer over a low heat, stirring, until the sugar has dissolved. Stir in the almond extract, brandy and mixed spice. In a separate bowl, mix the cornflour and water to form

a paste. Remove the saucepan from the heat, stir in the cornflour paste, then return to the heat and stir constantly until the mixture boils. Stir in the remaining cherries, then pour into the pastry case. Dot with the unsalted butter.

• Cut the remaining pastry into long strips about 1 cm/½ inch wide. Lay five strips evenly across the top of the filling. Now lay six strips widthways over them to form a lattice. Trim off the ends and seal the edges with water. Use your fingers to crimp around the rim. Brush the top with beaten egg to glaze.

• Cover with foil and bake for 30 minutes. Discard the foil, then bake for a further15 minutes or until the pastry is golden. Serve warm.

Pecan Pie

Serves 8

Pastry

225 g/8 oz plain flour, plus extra for dusting

115 g/4 oz butter, plus extra for greasing

2 tbsp caster sugar

Filling

85 g/3 oz butter

115 g/4 oz soft dark brown sugar

150 g/5½ oz golden syrup

2 large eggs, beaten

1 tsp vanilla extract

100 g/3½ oz pecan nuts, roughly chopped

Directions

• Preheat the oven to 200°C/400°F/Gas Mark 6.

• Grease a 23-cm/9-inch fluted tart tin.

• For the pastry, place the flour in a bowl and rub in the butter using your fingertips until it resembles fine breadcrumbs. Stir in the sugar and add enough cold water to mix to a firm dough. Wrap in clingfilm and chill for 15 minutes until firm enough to roll out.

• Roll out the dough on a lightly floured surface and use to line the prepared tart tin. Prick the base with a fork. Chill for 15 minutes.

• Place the tart tin on a baking tray, line the pastry with a sheet of baking paper and fill with baking beans or dried beans. Bake in the preheated oven for 10 minutes. Remove the paper and weights and bake for an additional 5 minutes. Reduce the oven temperature to 180°C/350°F/Gas Mark 4.

• For the filling, place the butter, brown sugar and golden syrup in a saucepan and heat gently until melted. Remove from the heat and quickly beat in the eggs and vanilla extract. Stir the pecan nuts into the mixture. Pour into the pastry case and bake in the preheated oven for 35–40 minutes until the filling is just set. Serve warm or cold.

Mississippi Mud Pie

Serves 8

Pastry

175 g/6 oz plain flour, plus extra for dusting

2 tbsp cocoa powder

115 g/4 oz unsalted butter, plus extra for
 greasing

2 tbsp caster sugar

1–2 tbsp cold water

Filling

175 g/6 oz unsalted butter

375 g/13 oz soft dark brown sugar

4 eggs, lightly beaten

25 g/1 oz cocoa powder, sifted

175 g/6 oz plain chocolate, broken into pieces

300 ml/10 fl oz single cream

Decoration

450 ml/16 fl oz double cream, whipped

Chocolate flakes

Directions

• Preheat the oven to 190°C/375°F/Gas Mark 5. Grease a 23-cm/9-inch round tart tin.

• To make the pastry, sift the flour and cocoa into a mixing bowl. Rub in the butter with your fingertips until the mixture resembles fine breadcrumbs. Stir in the sugar and enough cold water to mix to a soft dough. Wrap the dough in clingfilm and chill in the refrigerator for 15 minutes.

• Roll out the dough on a lightly floured surface and use to line the tin. Line with baking paper and fill with baking beans or dried beans. Bake in the preheated oven for 15 minutes. Remove from the oven and remove the paper and weights. Bake the pastry case for a further 10 minutes.

• To make the filling, beat the butter and brown sugar together in a bowl and gradually beat in the eggs with the cocoa. Melt the chocolate in a heatproof bowl set over a saucepan of gently simmering water, then beat it into the mixture with the single cream.

• Reduce the oven temperature to 160°C/325°F/Gas Mark 3. Pour the filling into the pastry case and bake in the preheated oven for 45 minutes or until the filling has set gently.

• Leave the pie to cool completely in the tin, then transfer to a serving plate. Cover with the whipped cream. Decorate with chocolate flakes and chill until ready to serve.

Key Lime Pie

Serves 8

Crumb Base

225 g/8 oz digestive biscuits, crushed

2 tbsp caster sugar

½ tsp ground cinnamon

85 g/3 oz butter, plus extra for greasing

Filling and Decoration

550 g/1 lb 4 oz sweetened condensed milk

125 ml/4 fl oz freshly squeezed lime juice

Finely grated rind of 3 limes

4 egg yolks

Whipped cream, to serve

Directions

- Preheat the oven to 160°C/325°F/Gas Mark 3.

- Lightly grease a 23-cm/9-inch round fluted tart tin.

- To make the crumb base, place the biscuits, caster sugar and cinnamon in a food processor and process until fine crumbs form. Do not overprocess to a powder. Add the melted butter and process again until combined.

- Tip the crumb mixture into the prepared tart tin and press over the base and sides. Place the tart tin on a baking tray and bake in the preheated oven for 5 minutes.

- Meanwhile, beat the condensed milk, lime juice, lime rind and egg yolks together in a bowl until well blended.

- Remove the tart tin from the oven, pour in the filling and spread out to the edges. Return to the oven for a further 15 minutes or until the filling is set around the edges but still wobbly in the centre.

- Leave to cool completely on a wire rack, then cover and chill for at least 2 hours. Serve spread thickly with freshly whipped cream.

Really Rich Chocolate Tartlets

Serves 8

Pastry

200 g/7 oz plain flour, plus extra for dusting

115 g/4 oz butter, cut into cubes, plus extra

  for greasing

2 tbsp icing sugar

1 egg yolk

2–3 tbsp cold water

Filling and Decoration

275 g/9¾ oz plain chocolate, broken

  into pieces

115 g/4 oz butter

60 g/2¼ oz icing sugar

300 ml/10 fl oz double cream

Grated chocolate, to decorate.

Directions

• Preheat the oven to 200°C/400°F/Gas Mark 6. Grease 8 x 10-cm/4-inch tartlet tins or line with baking paper.

• Place the flour in a large bowl. Add the butter and rub it in with your fingertips until the mixture resembles breadcrumbs. Add the icing sugar, egg yolk and enough water to form a soft dough. Cover and chill in the fridge for 15 minutes.

• Roll the dough out on a lightly floured work surface. Using a pastry cutter make 8 x 15-cm/6-inch rounds and line the tartlet tins. Chill for 30 minutes.

• Prick the base of the pastry with a fork and line with crumpled foil. Bake in the preheated oven for 10 minutes,

then remove the foil and bake for 5–10 minutes until crisp. Transfer to a wire rack to cool. Reduce the oven temperature to 160°C/325°F/Gas Mark 3.

• To make the filling, place the chocolate, butter and icing sugar in a heatproof bowl set over a saucepan of simmering water and heat until melted. Remove from the heat and stir in 175 ml/6 fl oz of the double cream.

• Remove the pastry cases from the tins and place on a baking tray. Fill each pastry case with the chocolate. Bake for 5 minutes. Cool, then chill until required.

• To serve, whip the remaining cream and pipe or spoon into the centre of each tart. Decorate with grated chocolate.

Fresh Blueberry Pie

Serves 8

Pastry

300 g/10½ oz plain flour, plus

    extra for dusting

Pinch of salt

75 g/2¾ oz butter, chilled and diced, plus

    extra for greasing

75 g/2¾ oz white vegetable fat,

    chilled and diced

1½ tsp white wine vinegar

5-6 tbsp iced water

Milk, to glaze

Filling

550 g/1 lb 4 oz fresh blueberries

85 g/3 oz caster sugar

25 g/1 oz cornflour

15 g/½ oz butter

Directions

• To make the pastry, sift the flour and salt into a large bowl. Add the butter and vegetable fat and rub into the flour until the mixture resembles fine breadcrumbs. Make a well in the centre and stir in the vinegar and enough of the iced water to mix to a firm dough. Wrap in clingfilm and chill in the refrigerator for 30 minutes.

• Preheat the oven to 220°C/425°F/Gas Mark 7. Place a baking sheet in the oven to preheat. Lightly grease a 23-cm/9-inch fluted pie dish.

• Roll two thirds of the pastry out on a lightly floured surface and use to line the pie dish. Trim the edges and prick the base all over with a fork. Chill in the refrigerator for 10 minutes.

• For the filling, mix the blueberries, sugar and cornflour in a bowl. Spoon the filling into the pastry case and dot with the butter.

• Roll the rest of the pastry out thinly on a lightly floured surface and cut into strips about 1-cm/½ -inch wide. Arrange in a lattice pattern over the filling. Trim the edges and seal them with a dab of cold water.

• Glaze the pastry lattice and rim with milk. Place the pie on the hot baking sheet and bake in the preheated oven for 40-45 minutes, or until the pastry is crisp and golden. Serve warm or cold.

Peach & Almond Pie

Serves 8

Pastry

115 g/4 oz plain chocolate, broken into pieces

200 g/7 oz plain flour, plus extra for dusting

115 g/4 oz unsalted butter, plus

   extra for greasing

25 g/1 oz ground almonds

Few drops almond extract

1–2 tbsp cold water

Glaze

4 tbsp peach (or apricot) jam

1 tbsp peach (or apricot) brandy

Filling

225 g/8 oz blanched almonds

100 g/3½ oz caster sugar

25 g/1 oz unsalted butter

2 egg yolks

4 egg whites

1 tsp almond extract

5–6 ripe peaches (or apricots)

Directions

- Preheat the oven to 190°C/375°F/Gas Mark 5.

- Grease a 23-cm/9-inch fluted tart tin.

- To make the pastry, melt the chocolate in a heatproof bowl set over a saucepan of barely simmering water. Remove from the heat and leave to cool slightly. Sift the flour into a bowl and rub in the butter with the fingertips until the mixture resembles breadcrumbs. Make a well in the centre and add the melted chocolate, ground almonds, almond extract and enough water to mix to a dough. Knead lightly. Wrap the dough in clingfilm and chill in the refrigerator for 30 minutes.

- Roll out the dough on a lightly floured surface and line the prepared tin.

- For the filling, process the blanched almonds and caster sugar in a food processor, until finely ground. Add the butter and process until smooth. Add the egg yolks, egg whites and almond extract and process until combined.

- Peel, halve and stone the peaches. Thinly slice the peach halves crossways. Spoon the almond mixture into the pastry case and arrange the peach slices on top, overlapping slightly.

- Bake in the preheated oven for 50 minutes or until set and golden brown.

- To make the glaze, heat the jam and brandy in a small saucepan, stirring until melted. Brush the glaze over the top of the pie and serve warm.

Three Berry Pie

Serves 8

Pastry

175 g/6 oz plain flour, plus extra for dusting

25 g/1 oz ground hazelnuts

115 g/4 oz butter, softened, plus

   extra for greasing

70 g/2½ oz caster sugar

Finely grated rind of 1 lemon

1 egg yolk, beaten

3 tbsp milk

Filling

200 g/7 oz fresh blueberries

200 g/7 oz fresh raspberries

200 g/7 oz fresh blackberries

3 tbsp caster sugar

2 tbsp milk, for brushing

Directions

- Preheat the oven to 190°C/375°F/Gas Mark 5. Grease a 23-cm/9-inch pie dish with butter.

- To make the pastry, sift the flour into a bowl, then add the hazelnuts. Rub in the butter with fingertips until the mixture resembles breadcrumbs, then sift in the caster sugar. Add the lemon rind, egg yolk and milk and mix.

- Turn out on to a lightly floured surface and knead briefly. Wrap in clingfilm and leave to chill in the refrigerator for 30 minutes.

- Roll out two thirds of the pastry to a thickness of 5 mm/ ¼ inch and use it to line the base and sides of the dish.

- To make the filling, place the fruits in a saucepan with the caster sugar and leave to simmer, stirring frequently, for 5 minutes. Remove the pan from the heat.

- Spoon the fruits into the pastry case. Roll out the remaining pastry to cover the pie. Trim and crimp around the edge, then make 2 small slits in the top and decorate with 2 leaf shapes cut out from the pastry trimmings. Brush with a little milk and bake in the preheated oven for 40 minutes or until the pastry is golden brown.

- Serve warm or cooled.

Chocolate Pumpkin Pie

Serves 8

Base

225 g/8 oz digestive biscuits, finely crushed

85 g/3 oz butter, melted, plus extra for
  greasing

1 tbsp caster sugar

2 tbsp soft light brown sugar

½ tsp salt

½ tsp ground cinnamon

40 g/1½ oz plain chocolate (at least 70%
  cocoa solids), chopped

Filling

125 g/4½ oz plain chocolate, broken into pieces

55 g/2 oz unsalted butter

425 g/15 oz canned pumpkin purée or puréed
  butternut squash

350 ml/12 fl oz evaporated milk

175 g/6 oz soft light brown sugar

3 large eggs

1 tbsp cornflour

2 tsp vanilla extract

1½ tsp salt

2 tsp mixed spice

Directions

• Preheat oven to 180°C/350°F/Gas Mark 4 and grease a 23-cm/9-inch pie dish.

• To make the base, combine the biscuit crumbs, butter, sugars, salt and cinnamon in a bowl. Firmly press the mixture into the base and up the sides of the pie dish. Bake for 8–10 minutes until firm.

• Remove from the oven and sprinkle the chopped plain chocolate over the base. Return to the oven for about 1 minute to melt the chocolate. Spread the chocolate in a thin layer on the base and up the sides. Leave to cool on a wire rack and reduce the oven temperature to 160°C/325°F/Gas Mark 3.

• To make the filling, melt the plain chocolate and butter in

a heatproof bowl set over a saucepan of simmering water, stirring until smooth. Remove from the heat.

• Mix the pumpkin purée, milk, brown sugar, eggs, cornflour, vanilla, salt and mixed spice in a medium bowl. Whisk one third of the pumpkin mixture into chocolate mixture. Whisk in remaining pumpkin mixture until completely incorporated.

• Transfer the pie dish to a baking tray and pour the pumpkin mixture into case. Bake in the preheated oven for 55–60 minutes until the centre is set but still a bit wobbly. Leave to cool on a wire rack.

• Refrigerate for at least 8 hours, but preferably overnight, until well chilled. Serve cold.

Lemon Sponge Pie

Serves 8

Pastry

butter for greasing

500 g/1lb 2 oz ready-made

   shortcrust pastry

flour for dusting

Filling

2 eggs

85 g/3 oz butter

200 g/7 oz caster sugar

2 tsp finely grated lemon rind

4 tbsp lemon juice

2 tbsp plain flour

Pinch of salt

225 ml/8 fl oz milk

Directions

- Preheat the oven to 220°C/425°F/Gas Mark 7. Grease a 23-cm/9-inch tart tin.

- Roll out the pastry on a lightly floured surface and use it to line the tart tin. Bake in the preheated oven for 8 minutes or until lightly browned. Leave to cool on a wire rack.

- To make the filling, separate the egg yolks from the whites. Place the whites in a bowl and set aside.

- Beat the butter in a large bowl with an electric mixer until fluffy. Add the caster sugar and beat until combined. Beat in the egg yolks, lemon rind, lemon juice, flour and salt until just combined. Add the milk and beat until just combined (the mixture will be thin and appear curdled).

- Whisk the egg whites in a separate bowl with an electric mixer until stiff peaks form. Fold the egg whites into the beaten mixture. Transfer the mixture to the pastry case. Loosely cover the top of the pie with foil to prevent overbrowning, taking care the foil does not touch the filling.

- Bake in the preheated oven for 10 minutes. Reduce the oven temperature to 180°C/350°F/Gas Mark 4 and bake for a further 20–25 minutes until the centre is solid and the thc top is slightly golden. Serve warm.

Index